17 JUN–18 JUL

APOLOGIA.

BY ALEXI KAYE CAMPBELL

Kristin Miller is a respected art historian. Her birthday should be a time for celebration but when her sons deliver their own versions of the past, everyone must confront the cost of Kristin's commitment to her passions.

APOLOGIA is Alexi Kaye Campbell's electrifying second play following his acclaimed debut **The Pride** (Laurence Olivier Award, Critics' Circle Award).

Direction **Josie Rourke** Design **Peter McKintosh**
Lighting **Hartley T A Kemp** Sound **Emma Laxton**

Box Office 020 8743 5050
www.bushtheatre.co.uk

bush theatre

supported by
h&f hammersmith & fulham

ARTS COUNCIL ENGLAND

wallace shawn season

the fever

2 April – 2 May

Clare Higgins delivers
Shawn's seminal play.

grasses of a thousand colours

12 May – 13 June

Miranda Richardson and
Wallace Shawn in his
explicit new play.

aunt dan and lemon

20 May – 27 June

Lemon (**Jane Horrocks**) hears
intimate secrets from Dan's
(**Lorraine Ashbourne**) exotic
adult world.

There will also be readings of the plays The Hotel Play, Our Late Night, A Thought in
Three Parts, Marie and Bruce and The Designated Mourner, as well as screenings of
the films My Dinner with André and Vanya on 42nd Street.

020 7565 5000
www.royalcourttheatre.com

THE CONTINGENCY PLAN

Steve Waters

'You know, when people suggest all sorts of cures for some disease or other, it means it's incurable. I keep thinking, racking my brains, and I come up with plenty of solutions, plenty of remedies, and basically, that means none – not one.'

Gaev in The Cherry Orchard, *Anton Chekhov*

For Doreen Chalmers
with thanks

The author would like to thank the following people for their help in developing this play: Dr Anna Jones, Dr Eric Wolf and Dr John King from British Antarctic Survey; all at Tipping Point, especially Peter Gingold; Jonathan Brearley from the Department of Climate Change and Energy; all my friends in HICCA; Stephen Meek; Dale Harrison and Rob Coleman from RSPB Titchwell; all the Bush Theatre especially Josie Rourke; George Gotts, Raz Shaw and Frances Poet for their work with me on *A Plague of People*; Tamara Harvey and Michael Longhurst for their close work on the text; and the cast of the first production for their tireless attention to detail.

ON THE BEACH

'The world is turnin'
Hope it don't turn away.'

'On the Beach', *Neil Young*

8

Characters

WILL, *a glaciologist, thirty-seven*
SARIKA, *a senior Civil Servant, thirty-three*
ROBIN, *an ex-glaciologist, sixty-seven*
JENNY, *his wife, sixty*

Setting

ACT ONE
Above a salt marsh, on Robin and Jenny's land in north-west Norfolk; April, Saturday

ACT TWO
The same; September, Saturday 8 p.m.

Time

The near future

This text went to press before the end of rehearsals and so may differ slightly from the play as performed.

ACT ONE

Scene One

Near ROBIN *and* JENNY*'s house looking out to sea. Mid-morning.*

ROBIN*'s looking through a telescope of considerable power on a tripod.*

He's in shabby yet attractive cut-off jeans; a plaid shirt, ripped; glasses on a chain around his neck; on his feet, battered trainers. He's wiry and weather-beaten and he moves fast. On a wind-up, battery-free stereo, a tape plays almost inaudibly Neil Young's 'On the Beach'. ROBIN checks the telescope, humming.

He notes something in a notepad.

ROBIN. Jen. It's back.

JENNY (*off*). What?

ROBIN. On the marsh. Jen!

JENNY (*off*). Where are you?

ROBIN. Down here. It's clearly on the marsh.

> JENNY *appears, breathless. She's a sixty-year-old; face devoid of make-up bar a little eyeliner; snowy long hair, dishevelled, piled up on top and held with a bandanna.*

JENNY. What are you talking about?

ROBIN. You see it? The cheek of it.

JENNY. I have no idea what you're talking about.

ROBIN. Way out of its range.

JENNY. Why, why are you listening to this out here?

> Why are you out here listening to this old rubbish?

JENNY silences the stereo. Immediately a wash of sound, the distant suck of surf, battling gulls, a dredger.

ROBIN. Look, look, out Brancaster way.

Governor's Point.

JENNY. I thought there was a trespasser or something.

ROBIN. You can see it. On Governor's Point.

JENNY reluctantly looks through the eyepiece of the telescope.

You see it now?

JENNY. No. Nothing.

ROBIN. You must see something.

JENNY. Nope.

ROBIN. See it now?

JENNY. No.

ROBIN refocuses it.

ROBIN. You surely see something.

JENNY. See my eyelashes.

ROBIN. Here then.

He adjusts the focus.

Lift it a little, a little.

You see Governor's Point, okay?

JENNY. Hang on. Okay. I see Governor's Point.

ROBIN. What do you notice about it?

JENNY. I notice as usual that Governor's Point is a great big lump of sand in the North Sea.

ROBIN. Ah. Maybe it's... maybe it's already – can I see?

He moves her aside.

Couldn't be a spoonbill.

JENNY. Okay. This is about birds.

ROBIN. Clearly not a grey heron.

JENNY. Up since God knows when because of a bird.

ROBIN. The phone woke me at five.

JENNY. And you didn't answer it?

Have you even had any breakfast?

ROBIN. Little egret.

They sense the warming. We know that.

But also they come inland as the seas get more turbulent.

JENNY. I don't have time for ornithology, Rob, I need to get to Lynn –

ROBIN. Is he there already?

JENNY. He left a garbled message from RAF Lyneham saying he 'might' be there mid-morning, it being Will, nothing more forthcoming than that.

ROBIN. So he's finally here. Everything's converging.

JENNY. Oh, Robin, Will's simply coming home for a refuel, it means nothing especially portentous, I doubt he'll stay longer than Monday.

ROBIN. Jenny, there's an event coming; it's building in the Atlantic; probably be with us by the small hours.

JENNY. The forecast's a cloudless day.

ROBIN. That bird knows it. Blown several latitudes north looking for landfall.

When it leaves again, it'll be time.

JENNY. Robin, any storm tonight'll be the accidental meeting of hot and cold air fronts, and if a little egret decides to patronise our marsh, a little egret patronises our marsh and those two matters are entirely unrelated.

I'd better get off.

Could you get his bedroom ready?

I've laid out something for lunch and, please please, when he comes, please, no talk of storms and birds and phases.

She looks at ROBIN.

God, it'll be good to see him.

ROBIN. Mmm.

JENNY. We're incomplete. Without him.

And I worry about him.

Stuck on that base in the middle of that nothingness.

Never meeting anyone, never travelling anywhere. A man in his thirties.

ROBIN. He has his work.

JENNY. Oh, he's got that all right.

ROBIN. Work of that urgency is pitiless. God, when I was at that pitch…

JENNY. Were you really the best of role models?

ROBIN. What?

JENNY. I sometimes wonder whether we harmed him, bringing him up that way?

ROBIN. Oh, Jenny, don't be daft. He's a magnificent specimen.

JENNY. Given he was always so bloody biddable. If he'd had a sibling at least.

ROBIN. He's just focused. Full of purpose. From the start it was clear what he was. This is the lad who classified his toys into organic and inorganic matter – right?

JENNY. Oh God. Fossils set out in the correct chronology. The egg museum.

ROBIN. Shaking me awake to look at the meteor shower.

JENNY. Had to take that telescope out of his bedroom, he barely slept.

ROBIN. If I said such things were God-given, I'd say he was God-given.

JENNY. I just feel his whole life, our whole life has been a preparation for an event that never arrives.

Pause.

ROBIN. Well. Okay. Maybe if I'd had half his tenacity, his application, letting nothing stand in the way of the work, nothing, we'd not be where we are now.

JENNY. Oh. Sorry. Did I... stand in your way?

ROBIN. Oh, Jen. Come on.

JENNY. I hope I didn't. Stand in your way.

ROBIN. You know you –

JENNY. Because if I ever thought – do you actually think that?

ROBIN. You don't need me to answer that.

JENNY. Don't I?

ROBIN. Jenny, he's coming home.

It can only mean one thing.

His work's complete.

And if his work's complete, then my work's complete.

JENNY. Right. What work is that, Rob?

ROBIN*'s back at the telescope.*

ROBIN. No, that's no spoonbill, the beak's all wrong. Look at him, mincing across the tidal mud.

JENNY *looks at him.*

JENNY. Okay. Fine.

I'll drive to Lynn. Pick up a few things.

You get his room ready.

She looks at him; then goes.

ROBIN. Yes, the forecast's clear.

Ridge of high pressure.

We can eat out here.

Watch the weather come in.

ROBIN *puts on his glasses, picks up his notepad. He waits.*

JENNY*'s car starts off;* ROBIN *heads into the house.*

A moment. From the other side of the stage, WILL *enters with* SARIKA; *they're both spattered with mud;* SARIKA*'s not dressed for the country, she's in a suit;* WILL *is in informal gear but is dealing with a wet shoulder bag with equipment in it, and also a rucksack.*

SARIKA. Look at these shoes.

WILL. Technically, you should wear wellies here.

SARIKA. You imagine I own a pair of wellies?

WILL. I'll get you some.

SARIKA. You will never see me in wellies.

The day you see me in wellies –

WILL. You could make wellies cool!

SARIKA. Oh, look at these shoes, they are – fucked.

She sits and takes them off.

Ugh – stink of eggs.

WILL. So. This is my… home.

SARIKA. Well… it's… lovely.

WILL. On a fine day, yes.

SARIKA. Gorgeous house.

WILL. Just a wreck when they came.

SARIKA. Could just sleep. Right here.

She lies back.

WILL. God!

SARIKA. What?

WILL. Sorry. You know it's just – your feet.

SARIKA. What?

WILL. It's just their... shape –

SARIKA. What?

WILL. They have a wonderful shape.

I never noticed before.

She laughs.

SARIKA. So you have a thing about feet?

WILL. Not feet in general, just your particular feet.

SARIKA. You freak, Will!

WILL. I take a purely scientific interest.

SARIKA. Kiss them then.

My athlete's foot. My verucas.

No. Kiss me. Kiss my mouth.

Pause. They kiss but he gets the giggles.

Is that so funny? What?

What is it?

WILL. Sorry.

SARIKA. What?

WILL. Nothing.

SARIKA. Tell me.

WILL. When I come back I kind of – I sort of get double vision – can't explain it. Like, just now, how many times, God, I fantasised about being with a girl – here. Like this.

SARIKA. Just fantasies?

WILL. Oh, shit, yeah. No girls in my childhood. Too busy measuring, I dunno, worm casts.

So thanks. For bringing me back.

SARIKA. Still think I should have taken you to my flat and ravished you.

But this is nice too.

WILL. Sshh!

SARIKA. What?

WILL. It's him.

SARIKA. God. They're in?

WILL. He never leaves this place.

SARIKA. Did he see – us?

WILL. Nah. Ranting away on the telephone. Jesus.

SARIKA. What's he so angry about? God, listen to him.

WILL. Ranting away. Oblivious.

SARIKA. Why's he never leave here?

He's an explorer, isn't he?

WILL. Yeah. Dad's a sort of human subglacial lake.

SARIKA. Sorry?

WILL. Unreachable, unsoundable, trapped between the seabed and the ice. Who knows what life forms swim in there?

SARIKA. Maybe you mystify him too much. Are people really so mysterious?

WILL. Compared with people, ice is a cinch.

Dad!

SARIKA. Leave him, leave him to it.

Let's have a dip. In that fabulous sea.

Look at it, turquoise, positively Caribbean.

WILL. Won't feel Caribbean when you're in it. Not in April.

SARIKA. You can get down from here?

WILL. The path goes down from there, through the dunes.

SARIKA. Man, your own path to the sea.

WILL. We let the odd birder in.

Can't fence off the beach.

But given it's a kind of promontory, marsh on each side, when the tide's in you have to come through the copse back there, right through the garden, which is not encouraged.

SARIKA. Let's go paddle.

She grabs her bag.

Shit, Will, look, this is absolutely bloody drenched.

WILL. Get the stuff out of it.

SARIKA. Everything's – totally – soaked.

She decants bits of equipment.

Fuck – the BlackBerry.

That's the Ministry's property!

WILL. Bad call.

'Government BlackBerry found in salt marsh.'

SARIKA. Whose idea was it to walk it!

WILL. Wasn't that particular idea yours?

Reckon the circuitry's wet.

Could probably get the back off and dry it.

SARIKA. Course you wouldn't have one.

No networks in Antarctica.

He fiddles with it with a little Philips screwdriver he pulls from his pocket.

We should've gone to my flat.

WILL. I'm sorry, I can get it dry –

SARIKA. I cannot be out of contact. Fuck!

WILL. Didn't your minister encourage you to take a break?

SARIKA. Sure, he insists on a mandatory twenty-four-hours'
    family time but he still expects me to mind the shop. Oh, and
    I was going to e-mail the review and circulate the – shit.
    Sorry, stressing –

WILL. It's okay – I shouldn't have –

SARIKA. No, sorry – kick the crackberry habit, kick it. Sorry.

WILL. 'Government BlackBerry in salt marsh.'

SARIKA. Okay. Very witty.

    Pause.

WILL. You told him about me yet?

SARIKA. God, no. Of course not.

    You're my WMD.

    To be deployed strategically. On Monday.

WILL. Monday! Of course.

SARIKA. I said we'd move fast.

    Chris claims he's easing his way into the post but we're
    doodling, bottom of the agenda at Cabinet, everything's
    banks and capitalisation and social policy and that's nastier
    than I thought. Climate change is clearly sorted.

    You're going to change that. Bring home the bad news.

WILL. Yeah. I mean, I hope I can, okay, help.

SARIKA. It's the event you predicted that will clinch it, the
    massive event? That's what we need now, that kind of
    focusing threat. Monday'll define the broad thrust of policy.
    Jenks'll give the keynote and if we don't watch out he'll set
    the tone for the day. God, I really cannot wait to see his face
    when you walk in. All set to jump on his Stability Theory.

WILL. Stability Hypothesis.

    Sorry.

SARIKA. Yes, yes.

She laughs.

Never forget I'm broad brush.

I'll offer context, sketch in the stuff about Jenks and your dad, measuring ice streams and glacier motion on the West Antarctic Ice Sheet. You elucidate what that means.

WILL. Well, they confirmed the ice sheet stable, that it tended to stability and that any warming, and they noted some, was just the long melt of the last ice age.

SARIKA. Hence the infamous Stability Hypothesis?

WILL. Yep: stubborn as a drumlin, you can't go over it, you can't go under it, it's irrefutable, and it's beautiful actually.

SARIKA. And just to get this clear in my muddy mind, it says, in effect, no rise in global temperature within any conceivable range can melt the largest mass of ice in the world – words to that...

WILL. Basically it claims the West Antarctic is impregnable.

SARIKA. But now (fanfare, drum roll), here's the man who's proved the exact opposite – that in fact the Western Antarctic Ice Sheet is on the verge of collapse; that in fact sea-level rises of minimum five metres are imminent; and that in fact we are on the brink of a catastrophic event.

WILL. Wait, wait – Sarika –

SARIKA. What? I was just bigging you up –

WILL. Just because the Hypothesis flies in the face of current ice behaviour doesn't mean we can actually disprove the fucker.

SARIKA. But that's what you've done?

WILL. That's what I set out to do.

And thus far have failed. To do.

SARIKA. Right. Sorry, did I misunderstand the imminence... of the breakthrough?

WILL. I don't think I ever suggested I was Nostradamus. Did I? I mean, I'm here to talk about my work, yes, about science, yes. But there's no way I can offer the kind of certainty you seem to be asking for. On Monday.

SARIKA. But you know the ice sheet's in a critical state, right?

WILL. The melt's exponential.

SARIKA. Okay, so even if you can't prove it, you know it so you have to say it –

WILL. Sarika, do you have, like, rules in your family? Unspoken rules?

SARIKA. Sorry?

WILL. No one ever actually lays them down, no one ever explicitly says, you know, these are the rules; but you learn them. Like here the rules are:

Birds are more important than humans.

Never believe anything said by a politician.

Never ask about the past.

Never discuss anything without the data.

SARIKA. Will, if I bided by my family rules I'd be a GP in Lutterworth with a husband who smells of cumin. You break your rules, don't you?

WILL. I could break one, maybe two.

If I say what you want with what I know I'll break the whole fucking lot.

Pause.

SARIKA. There's this thing I was going to show you. Promise not to take it the wrong way. Do you promise? Not to take it the wrong way?

WILL. Okay. I mean, I don't know.

She reaches into her bag, rifles through to find an envelope.

SARIKA. Crap, this is wet too.

Got a colleague in the archives to look up stuff. On Colin.

About his work, his past.

WILL. Right. Why?

SARIKA. Why? Because he's a deadweight.

WILL. Is that ethical?

SARIKA. Did I say I was ethical?

Okay, and also, also about – your father.

WILL. What?

SARIKA. Can I be frank? The story you tell, this story about
    your father, it doesn't make sense. Robin and Jenks prove the
    Stability Hypothesis, but for some reason your dad doesn't
    publish, doesn't sign the paper, isn't mentioned in Jenks's
    acknowledgements even. That's pretty weird, isn't it?
    Leaving aside the fact that your father then exits altogether
    from science, quits his job, steps out of – well, out of life. So
    I know this is presumptuous of me and if I were you I would
    be, would feel – pissed off – Will.

But I don't like mysteries, you know, I like stories to have a
    clear resolution.

And here's a mystery. Look.

He opens the envelope, to look at the document within.

WILL. This is what – classified – what?

SARIKA. Declassified now.

WILL. What's the relevance of this?

SARIKA. It's the only record of a meeting between a polar
    scientist and the then Minister for Science and Education,
    one Margaret Thatcher. Subject: 'The Contingency Plan.'
    Which is incredibly interesting.

I mean, with reference to what, why would a polar scientist
    be granted an audience with a minister back then?

WILL. Names blacked out.

Contents blacked out.

Dad wouldn't be seen dead talking to a politician, any politician.

SARIKA. When exactly did your father come back from Antarctica?

WILL. 1974.

SARIKA. You're sure about that?

WILL. This is, what, '73.

Couldn't be him. Or Jenks. Jenks came back, published '74.

SARIKA. You're completely sure about that?

Pause.

I'm really handling this well.

Some Machiavel I am.

Shall I take that – ?

WILL *folds up the document, puts it in his pocket.*

WILL. See that ash tree – by the lagoon?

There? Dead one?

Used to climb it, built myself a house, 'the lab' I called it. Flowered, annually. Used to be festooned with nests.

One night of not especially fierce winds it split, it broke off from its base. Couldn't work it out. Everything else survived the night, but my tree went down. Made no sense at all. Checked it out, the fallen trunk, peeled back the bark, looked inside and where there should have been layer on layer of wood, layering up the years of growth, there was nothing, nothing but dust, powder, parasites, shit. Must have been dead for years, dead from within.

He looks at her.

Do you see what I'm saying?

SARIKA. Will, you scared me, you dazzled me, you shook me awake and now, now you're going to dazzle Jenks, scare the

crap out of Chris, get 'Climate Change' written in neon on every policy and every statement and every Bill – and, forgive me, I happen to think that's more important now than dotting the 'i's on some data. And okay, if I'm wrong tell me to fuck off and I will, I'll just –

He kisses her almost breathlessly.

Phew! Shit.

WILL. Yeah. Sorry.

SARIKA. No. Do it again.

WILL. I think I better go in.

SARIKA. Okay.

WILL. On my own. Don't want to induce a coronary.

SARIKA. No.

Okay, I'll go and… paddle. Or something.

WILL. Right. It'll be cold.

SARIKA. Maybe I want to feel that cold.

WILL. Can you swim?

SARIKA. Can I swim? What do you think?

WILL. I don't know.

SARIKA. You think Asian girls don't swim?

WILL. No, don't be –

SARIKA. You are looking at the breaststroke champion of Rugby High School for Girls here, three years running.

WILL. I'd like to see your breaststroke.

SARIKA. Oh, you will see it.

You're going to see all kinds of stuff.

She kisses him, gathers her shoes, and wanders off.

WILL *alone. He looks at the document, sits. Rubs his face.*

Notices the stereo, switches it on, listens to the music.

ROBIN *enters from the house, looking thunderous; the sight of his son disarms him; he watches him for a moment.*

ROBIN. Am I dreaming?

WILL. What is this?

Let me guess: singer-songwriter, lonely wheedling voice, self-pitying – in this case, Canadian self-pity…

Let's see. '75?

ROBIN. '74.

WILL. '74. What is it about you and 1974?

ROBIN. Vintage year. For music.

WILL. Yeah. And for me.

ROBIN. Where's Jen?

WILL. Neil Young!

ROBIN. Correct.

WILL. 'After the Goldrush'?

ROBIN. 'On the Beach'.

WILL. Why are you listening to that?

ROBIN. Neglected masterpiece.

WILL. Justly neglected.

He switches it off.

ROBIN. Jen was picking you up.

WILL. Well, we got a cab.

ROBIN. 'We'?

WILL. Walked the last bit through the marsh.

What happened to the raised path?

ROBIN. Yeah, I need to get to that.

WILL. Do I stink as bad as I think I stink?

ROBIN. Smell like a diver's jockstrap.

They laugh.

WILL. Well. Come here, then.

They embrace, belatedly.

ROBIN. Oh, look at you. Entirely real!

WILL. Don't feel very real right now.

ROBIN. Pale. Got that wintered-out look.

WILL. Yeah – rapid re-entry and that.

ROBIN. Back with the earthlings, eh?

WILL. It's weird. Good.

ROBIN. Just to smell stuff again.

WILL. Hear stuff.

ROBIN. Yeah. Remember all that.

Pause.

WILL. Practically had to shut my eyes and ears on the train – too bright, too loud, too much colour, too many people.

ROBIN. Yeah, well, you've been in the world as it should be and now you're back in the world as it is.

Nice though, for us earthlings to see you, y'know.

WILL. Likewise, you Neanderthal old fuck.

ROBIN. Ah, where's his deference these days?

WILL. All gone, mate, all of it.

ROBIN. And did you get taller? Is that possible?

WILL. You're just shorter. Shrinkage.

ROBIN. Don't talk to me about shrinkage.

You lose your hair, your height, your libido, your pension's value, your standing in life. Not good being old.

He lets WILL *go; looks at him.*

I was surprised. When you said you were coming.

WILL. That was the idea.

ROBIN. You were doing the winter.

WILL. Well, yeah, I was.

ROBIN. That's why I was surprised.

Being as it's April.

WILL. I know it's April, Dad.

ROBIN. Forgive me, Will, you're not short-changing the
research?

WILL. I think I know how to do my own research.

ROBIN. Yeah. Course. So you did the instrument drop – on the
Bellingshausen Sea?

WILL. Okay. Right. Janey's seeing that through.

The team, I have a team of five, the team are seeing it
through.

ROBIN. Okay. So Janey's what, a – ?

WILL. Janey's a highly regarded meteorologist.

ROBIN. Good, good, 'cos you really need those temperature
measurements.

WILL. It's covered, Dad.

ROBIN. Sure, sure. Sorry. And how's the Brunt doing?

WILL. The Brunt. Okay. The Brunt is thinning. But still pretty
thick.

ROBIN. The Brunt has always been particularly vulnerable.

WILL. You found that, did you?

ROBIN. And, yes, you'll get thinning.

But thinning is perfectly compatible with stability.

WILL. Right.

The ice flows are exponentially faster on the West Antarctic
Ice Sheet. It's mental.

ROBIN. You have hard data for that?

WILL. A huge body of data.

ROBIN. Presumably it varies regionally?

WILL. Pine Island Glacier's at forty per cent increased motion; ice shelves are weakening everywhere; overall temperatures are up a full degree since '57.

ROBIN. But I suppose that'll be balanced out by the longer-term cooling data. On Pine Island.

WILL. That data doesn't make sense. To me.

ROBIN. You're not challenging our data collection?

WILL. Did you do Pine Island, or Colin?

ROBIN. I forget. I mean – both of us.

WILL. Those three years of cooling cut right across the pattern.

ROBIN. A pattern you're imposing on the data.

A pattern you'd like to see in the data.

WILL. We know it experienced warming in the sixties, the eighties.

The Stability Hypothesis rests heavily on Pine Island.

If that data didn't exist I could smash it to bits.

ROBIN. Did I teach you to rely on wishful thinking? That cooling data was arrived at through meticulous study.

No computing shortcuts, no modelling, no mooning over ice cores.

WILL. Right. Right…

Dad, do you think you could run to a welcoming hot drink, HobNob, cup of nettle tea?

ROBIN. You don't like nettle tea.

WILL. I was being sarcastic. Forget it.

ROBIN. What?

WILL. Forget the welcoming hot drink.

ROBIN. Have you written your findings in a paper?

WILL. How could I if I don't have the conclusive data?

ROBIN. If you don't have the fucking data, what on earth are you doing here talking to me?

Pause.

WILL. Might have had other reasons to come back.

ROBIN. No, Will, no, you absolutely have to complete the research before you speak to anyone. Anyone. You have to be note perfect.

WILL. Like you were?

ROBIN. What?

WILL. What do you want from me? Do you want me to vindicate you or to fail to vindicate you or what?

ROBIN. What I want is immaterial.

WILL. You still stand by the Hypothesis?

ROBIN. Where's the evidence not to?

WILL. But you never claimed it, never published on it.

ROBIN. Authorship is irrelevant.

Nobody owns the truth. Your task is to make sure it's robust and if it's not, fine, demolish it, demolish it, nothing would please me more than to be proved, utterly proved wrong.

WILL. Well, that seems to be beyond me, Dad, sorry.

ROBIN. Nothing's beyond you, Will, believe me.

WILL. All I know is that bastard is melting.

Melting fast, faster than you ever said, well, Jenks ever said and pretty soon we're going to feel the effects right here.

ROBIN. But that's just not good enough, is it, Will?

WILL *glares at* ROBIN; *then through the telescope.*

WILL. Yeah, thought I saw an egret in the marsh. Lovely bird.

In its habitat. Looks a bit of a twat here.

Is it me or is the sea closer?

Governor's Point's smaller.

Don't have the data, of course, so…

ROBIN. Shot to shit in the last storm.

Another one due tonight.

WILL. Nah. Something nasty in the Atlantic maybe. Should be fine here.

ROBIN. Oh, it'll come here too.

Over the marsh.

WILL. Over the marsh? What about the groins there. The dyke.

ROBIN *gives a low laugh.*

Don't be all spooky, Dad.

You don't suit spooky.

ROBIN. Tonight will a big one.

Tonight could be another '53.

WILL. It'll happen. But not tonight. The Environment Agency would have had you out of here.

ROBIN. They said that too, when I called them. I talk to them every day. They have a girl they put on me.

WILL. And what do they say?

ROBIN. Always the same thing. Only so many ways of saying you've thrown in the towel.

He laughs darkly.

They call it managed retreat, but if I was the sea I'd see it more as an undignified rout.

WILL. Dad, come on.

ROBIN. Done one of those, what are they, cost-benefit analyses and they said, well, there's only a couple of old tossers and birders and widowed ladies on that stretch of land (course never mention our bittern, the bearded tits, the Brent geese, couldn't fit that on the spreadsheet) –

WILL. They don't do it on a spreadsheet, Dad.

ROBIN. Brave talk about managing the human cost, which presumably'll mean the offer of a council house in Heacham currently occupied by Lithuanians.

WILL. Well, I'm sorry.

ROBIN. No need to be sorry, lad. It's for the best. The sea will prevail. It's Phase Four as anticipated.

WILL. The thing is the logic, the logic is infallible, this is going to happen all over – what do you mean, 'Phase Four'?

ROBIN. Let's go in, have some coffee, a nip of something, I think we've got carrot cake or ginger cake or –

WILL. Dad, there's stuff I need to tell you, I need to ask you –

ROBIN. Yes?

SARIKA *comes back on, her feet wet, her trousers rolled up.*

SARIKA. I trod on something sharp –

ROBIN. Who's this? Hey, what are you –

WILL. Sar, this is Sarika, Sar, this is –

SARIKA. Oh, I am so sorry, I didn't – I trod on –

WILL. Might be a weaver fish.

SARIKA. Really painful.

ROBIN. You don't have a permit to –

WILL. No, Dad, no, this, this is –

ROBIN. You're aware this is a site of scientific –

SARIKA. No, sorry, it's okay, I'm with –

WILL. Dad, the thing is I know –

ROBIN. No, this is private, protected –

SARIKA. I'm sorry, has Will not yet –?

WILL. We haven't had a chance –

ROBIN. Wait, wait, you know her – Will?

WILL. Dad, yeah, if you just shut up for a –

ROBIN. You, you know Will?

SARIKA. I'm his, well, he's my – this really hurts!

ROBIN. You know her?

JENNY *comes in from the house.*

JENNY. There's no bloody petrol in the Volvo, it ran out, on the track and I cannot find the key for the – camper – what's –

WILL. Mum. Hey. Sorry, I didn't – you got something for a weaver-fish sting?

JENNY. Sorry, you – what's this – ?

SARIKA. Ow ow – sorry, my foot's gone numb!

ROBIN. He – he came home. I don't know – she –

WILL. Early. Yeah. Sorry. Let me see it, stand still –

JENNY. Will, you're –

WILL. Have we got some ice or Salvesen –

JENNY. Sorry, who's this?

WILL. Yeah. And this is –

SARIKA. Are you Jenny? Hello, Jenny.

I hurt my foot on the beach.

Sorry. I've heard a lot about you. And you, of course, Robin.

I thought maybe, Will, maybe he'd – but clearly he hasn't had the opportunity.

Look, I'm sorry, I've been in the sea and I am actually really very cold and my foot is really hurting. Will!

WILL. Sorry, Sar, I should have –

Sarika – hang on – hang on. I'll show you – sorry, Mum, I –

He kisses JENNY, *takes* SARIKA *into the house.*

JENNY. Will!

ROBIN. He saw it. Will. He saw the egret.

Blackout.

Scene Two

Later.

Dusk above the marsh. It's calm.

There's a long trestle table with a hurricane lamp on it.

JENNY *is laying a large white cloth on it. She then lays it with cutlery and glasses;* WILL *is washing and dipping razor clams in hot water.*

JENNY. We're down to four tonnes per annum.

WILL. How could you possibly know that, Mum?

JENNY. With one of those carbon-calculator thingies.

WILL. And what is the data? That you input into the thingy?

JENNY. Don't get boringly scientific about it.

You enter in, you know, food miles –

WILL. Define 'food miles'.

JENNY. Oh, you know very well what I mean by food miles.

WILL. Yeah, but how does this thingy convert food miles into emission data.

JENNY. They know, they have a method for it.

WILL. 'They' being…?

JENNY. Of course, it's probably approximate, okay!

WILL. Oh, well, if it's approximate.

JENNY. Oh, air travel, that's a factor –

WILL. Air travel! You never fly!

JENNY. Well, precisely.

WILL. You never fly because you're afraid of flying.

JENNY. It doesn't go into your motivation – oh, frequency of car use, err, use of renewables, and given all, that I think we are definitely a tonne lighter this year, as a household, and I'll keep getting it down a tonne year on year until we get to zero!

WILL. Listen, when you get to zero emissions you're dead.

JENNY. As near as, then.

WILL. Although, of course, the process of decomposition will make you a net emitter of methane which is a far more virulent greenhouse gas than CO2.

JENNY. Well, I doubt they extend the exercise to the dead. And that's just bloody tasteless.

WILL. Sorry.

JENNY. Do you know what it was that got us down from five tonnes?

WILL. Dad refrained from his weekly bath?

JENNY. We stopped buying processed food – altogether. No tins, no packaging, no precooked stuff.

WILL. So, no Ambrosia Creamed Rice? I have been dreaming of Ambrosia Creamed Rice.

JENNY. Everything you will eat tonight I have sourced locally or grown myself – gathered the razor clams, picked the sea-kale for greens –

WILL. Sea-kale? That's chock-full of toxins.

JENNY. It just needs thorough, careful boiling.

WILL. Sadly the wine's from Chile.

JENNY. Couldn't you have got something more local?

WILL. Yeah, well, it was local. In Chile.

JENNY. I know you think it's highly comical.

WILL. No, no, in itself I think it's admirable.

JENNY. This is grass-roots stuff, no one leads, we don't wait
    for the politicians or the – because, like Gandhi said, 'Be the
    change you want to see.' Or was that Martin Luther King?

WILL. And who's this 'we' exactly?

JENNY. You promise not to laugh at me.

WILL. I'll promise but I'll probably fail.

JENNY. If you laugh I'll crown you.

WILL. Look, I am stony-faced.

JENNY. Okay.

   North Norfolk Area Climate Change Action.

WILL. North Norfolk Area what?

JENNY. Okay, bit of a mouthful admittedly and a lousy acronym.

WILL. Oh. 'NNACCA.'

JENNY. Yeah, you're breaking your promise now.

WILL. No, okay, NNACCA.

JENNY. But you know what it's like here, normally you don't
    speak to a soul in weeks, now we're going into schools,
    meeting with parish councillors, even the WI, seriously, they
    are the lynchpin, cake bakes, low-carbon cookbooks, the
    church, they screened the Al Gore three times –

WILL. Does Gore get royalties for that?

JENNY. Gore's film, Leonardo de Niro's film.

WILL. DiCaprio. I think.

   He's laughing.

   And when Keira Knightley makes hers you'll screen that too.

JENNY. Don't laugh at my life, Will. Leave that to your father.

Pause. WILL stops what he's doing.

WILL. I'm sorry. Hey. Mum. I am sorry.

SARIKA *comes in from the house.*

SARIKA. Quaint local customs in action, right?

WILL. Yeah. Shucking razor clams.

SARIKA. God, how totally exotic. Move over, Ray Mears.

WILL. Who's Ray Mears?

SARIKA. Forget it. Do they have wireless here?

WILL. Mum'll know.

JENNY. Wireless? Yes, yes, we do.

SARIKA. Oh, okay, can I get the password to…?

WILL. Mum? What's your password?

JENNY. Oh. I used to know that. What is it?

Oh, something… you could always use Rob's.

The line's intermittent anyway.

Broadband's still rather novel round here.

SARIKA. He's busy on his –

JENNY. He's meant to be watching the greens.

SARIKA. He said he's good at multitasking.

JENNY. The one thing he is incapable of is multitasking – oh, yes, something, something to do with seabirds.

WILL. There's a surprise.

JENNY. Fulmar, fulmar one!

SARIKA. Fulmar what?

JENNY. Rob'll know it. Fulmar one – yes. Maybe not.

It'll come to me.

SARIKA. So, something to do with fulmars.

JENNY. Could you take these in to Rob?

To be cooked in the wine.

SARIKA. Lovely.

She takes in a bowl of clam steaks.

WILL. This is hard work.

JENNY. I needed a tonne of salt to get them out of the sand.

WILL. Stubborn insular buggers.

JENNY. Remind you of anyone?

They laugh.

How old is Sarika? It is Sarika?

WILL. Why do you ask?

JENNY. I'm simply interested.

WILL. Yes, but what is the relevance of her age?

JENNY. I'm just asking, William, it's just an innocuous motherly question.

WILL. I don't actually know how old she is.

JENNY. You don't know how old she is, love?

WILL. No. Sorry. Thought it ungentlemanly to inquire.

This bastard won't open.

JENNY *grunts.*

JENNY. And may I ask how you met or is that an official secret too?

WILL. We met at Rothera.

JENNY. You can't have.

WILL. What do you mean?

JENNY. That girl's far too pretty to be a scientist.

WILL. Are scientists by definition ugly?

JENNY. Why would she be in Antarctica if she's not a scientist?

SARIKA *re-enters*.

WILL. No good?

SARIKA. Robin said it was something to do with terns. And anyway, he's crashed.

And there was nothing on the radio about any incipient storms. The Met Office would've flagged it by now.

WILL. Dad said it would come in from the west.

SARIKA. That's not reckoned to amount to much.

Do they – Jenny, do you get cable?

JENNY. Cable?

WILL. Can you imagine them having cable?

SARIKA. I could do with calling someone in the Department at least, getting them on it.

WILL. Is the landline…?

SARIKA. It's down. Apparently.

JENNY. We get a terrible service. Puff of wind in Hunstanton and it's gone.

Have my mobile.

WILL. You have a mobile!

JENNY. Did I not say? I never use it.

I think I have used it once. I want you to teach me how to text.

Don't let Rob know.

I got it in case he – you know.

Generally it doesn't work, but if you go up to the rise back towards the approach road, occasionally you get an intermittent signal.

Here. That's my number on the back there.

You could key in yours!

WILL. This is such progress, Mum.

SARIKA. Thanks, Jenny. I'll do that. Can I give them the number?

JENNY. Why not?

WILL. I'll come with you.

SARIKA. No. You need to talk to your mum about me, I expect.

JENNY. Blood from a very dry stone, Sarika.

SARIKA. Anyway, I can always scream, can't I?

JENNY. Dinner should be ready soon.

SARIKA. Ten minutes – just to check in.

She kisses WILL; JENNY *watches them.* SARIKA *goes.*
JENNY *sorts through* WILL's *remaining clams, discarding any excess.*

JENNY. Presumably she didn't arrive in the Antarctic by accident.

WILL. Oh. The inquisition continues. No.

Fact-finding visit.

JENNY. Ah! She's a journalist! I knew it.

WILL. Wrong again.

Look, if you need her CV I can e-mail it to you.

JENNY. If you won't tell me anything, love…

I mean, this must have been a while ago –

WILL. January, I think. Yes.

JENNY. January? You've told us nothing for three months?

WILL. I wanted to tell you in person, okay?

You don't seem very pleased.

JENNY. Pleased! Pleased? You idiot, of course I'm pleased, I'm
  – cock-a-hoop!

WILL. Yeah, but you never approve of –

JENNY. When do I ever get to meet them? By the time I hear
  about them they're history –

  You don't know girls, Will, you're an innocent.

  Robin's the same. The whole concept of the female sex
  defeats him and you – fact-finding for who?

WILL. For the Government. She's a Civil Servant.

  She works for the Department of Climate Change and Energy.

  Pause.

  Why the long pause?

JENNY. Have you told Robin?

WILL. Not yet.

JENNY. Don't.

WILL. It'll come out.

JENNY. Don't.

  He's in a very delicate place –

WILL. He seems a little more up actually.

JENNY. 'Up'! Hyper more like.

WILL. Excited.

JENNY. Which cannot be good.

WILL. I think it is good. I think it's good that he's thinking again.

JENNY. Look, he's very fragile, okay?

WILL. If we treat him like Delftware, he'll snap just as easy.

JENNY. You know what he's like.

  Any shift in the weather, the slightest thing, he is incapable
  of getting it in proportion, striding about, making
  calculations about sea-level rise, you know what he's like.

WILL. Well. Maybe that's not so irrational.

JENNY. Of course it's irrational.

WILL. I don't know.

Perhaps you should think about moving.

JENNY. What? What do you mean?

WILL. I dunno, inland even as far as Downham, Swaffham, I
dunno –

JENNY. What are you talking about?

WILL. Just a smaller place, inland, house'd go for a good sum –

JENNY. What, with the survey we'll get?

We can't even get insured these days.

And there's no reason to move.

This is our home. Your home.

WILL. Well. Maybe we can't assume homes any more.

JENNY. Will, if it wasn't for this place, Robin wouldn't have
stirred from his bed in thirty years.

WILL. He tells himself this. And I'm sorry, Mum, but you
conspire with it.

JENNY. What do you mean, I 'conspire', what the hell do you
mean by that?

I drove him here through a blizzard. Five months gone with
you. Yes, I'd come back from the maternity clinic and found
him sat on the floor of his room at Trinity, sat on the floor.
Couldn't face lunch. A man who'd walked, roped up,
through a sixty-knot wind in zero visibility.

Couldn't face lunch. You were kicking inside me, Will;
almost lost you there and then. I walked him through the
quad, packed him in our Escort, drove up the A10, to get to
the sea. And the next day he refused to leave, I pleaded with
him to go back. Flat refused.

It wasn't about here, it wasn't pretty that day, the sky like zinc, but no, still he said no going back; no more academia, no more science. And you think I should have dissuaded him? You think I wanted this to happen? Income gone in a trice, me having to find work, you barely weaned, this house a shell –

WILL. Mum, he was the best glaciologist of his day. The absolute works.

Comes home from Antarctica. Never goes back.

JENNY. Well, he changed tack.

WILL. Oh, right, develops this passion for birds, for Norfolk, for reclamation – because of this mysterious breakdown? Something must have induced it.

JENNY. It was nothing to do with science and everything to do with human frailty.

WILL. It must have been something to do with science.

JENNY. Will, you have to understand that he cannot, he must not go back there, to that time.

WILL. That time's coming to him one way or the other.

JENNY. What do you mean?

WILL. Hang on – he came back in January, right, and this, when –

JENNY. What?

WILL. When you came here.

JENNY. February.

WILL. February – no, it must have been earlier.

JENNY. It was February, yes, it was Valentine's Day –

WILL. But you said you were, how many months pregnant with me? Five?

JENNY. Oh. Yes.

WILL. And he couldn't have come home before, it wasn't easy to come home then, it was a major –

JENNY. What is this about?

WILL. I was conceived in October, right?

JENNY. I don't know – okay. Okay. Look, all I'm asking –

ROBIN *enters with a tray of plates. The others stand frozen.*

ROBIN. All you're asking is what, Jen?

JENNY. Nothing.

ROBIN. No, you were, you were asking for something.

JENNY. The sea-kale. I was asking where you'd got to... with the sea-kale.

ROBIN. Really?

JENNY. It shouldn't cook for more than five minutes.

ROBIN. Yeah, well... the kale's off.

JENNY. What?

ROBIN. I'm all for sea-kale in theory, but in practice it's a rubbery bitch of a brassica.

JENNY. You boil hard and you watch the water.

ROBIN. Oh, got it bubbling away, should have seen the micro-organisms coming off it, water ink-black and then it all shrivelled to buggery –

JENNY. But we don't have any other greens.

ROBIN. It's fine. I found a tin of peas.

JENNY. That tin's prehistoric.

I wanted something fresh for him, he's eaten nothing but tinned –

ROBIN. I daresay they were fresh when they were picked. You okay with peas, Will? You all right?

WILL *nods.*

How about... sorry, lost her name?

WILL. Sarika.

ROBIN. She okay with peas?

SARIKA *enters*.

SARIKA. I love peas. Frozen, tinned, whatever.

ROBIN. Good. Go with this little – what's your wine there?

WILL. God knows.

ROBIN. Sancerre. Yeah, peas go with that okay.

WILL. How's the weather?

SARIKA. Just bad, not disastrous, unfortunately.

Meant to dissipate north of Cornwall.

WILL. And what about thingy – Chris?

SARIKA. Not to be disturbed.

JENNY *picks up the wine, pours it out.* ROBIN *doles out the clams and peas. Through the next section they eat.*

ROBIN. Chris? Who's Chris?

SARIKA. Oh. Christopher Casson.

JENNY. One of Sarika's colleagues.

ROBIN. Heard the name. Celebrity chef?

Disc jockey?

SARIKA. He's new to politics.

ROBIN. Politics. Casson?

Why are we talking about him?

SARIKA. Minister for Climate Change. And Energy.

ROBIN. Ah! Hallelujah. A Minister for Climate Change. Well, we're saved. We can all relax and go home now.

SARIKA. Yes, I've heard that's how we're viewed round here.

JENNY. Right, anyone for clams? Harvested by yours truly today. Lovely with parmesan.

We try and source as much as possible from the vicinity.

ROBIN. What could she possibly mean by that, Will?

WILL. Ask her yourself, she's sat next to you.

SARIKA. Will tells me you take a sceptical line on politics.

ROBIN. We don't suffer any reverence here for certain mass delusions – the media, what passes for education, politics.

JENNY. I wish you could have had the sea-kale.

Despite the name it's not at all stringy –

WILL. Politics in itself shouldn't be a dirty word, should it? I mean, if we take politics to mean making a difference.

ROBIN. Why would we take it to mean that, mate?

SARIKA. Robin, do you not know what I do?

JENNY. How do you find the clams?

A bit chewy, some of them. A bit salty.

ROBIN. Salty indeed. No, what do you do, Sarina?

WILL. Sarika, Dad.

SARIKA. Fine. It's an odd name. Call me Sar.

WILL. Sarika's a senior Civil Servant. Fastest promotion to her grade ever.

JENNY. Good pensions apparently.

ROBIN. Civil Servant?

Nah, you're kidding me. Far too pretty.

SARIKA. That's a bit of a backhanded compliment.

ROBIN. What department? Culture?

SARIKA. Why would you think that, Robin?

Do I look excessively cultured or something?

ROBIN. You're not an economist.

WILL. She absolutely could be.

ROBIN. Not a scientist.

WILL. She's –

SARIKA. Will, thank you! I am actually. A biochemist.

By training.

ROBIN. Don't look like the biochemists I knew.

Tend to have beards.

SARIKA. Well. I shaved mine off.

ROBIN *laughs loudly.*

ROBIN. Ha! Good. Good.

SARIKA. Well. Okay. There is a ministry dedicated to climate change.

I, in effect, run it, well, carry out the minister's wishes.

ROBIN. Dedicated – what, to implementing climate change? Rolling out those CO2 quotas, laying the roads, getting those jets airborne.

SARIKA. You're really not going to take me seriously, are you? Which is fine.

ROBIN. I take you very seriously. You're a friend of Will's.

WILL. Government has to have some role in mitigating or adapting –

ROBIN. What do governments know? They don't have the knowledge.

WILL. They work with experts –

ROBIN. Experts, Will?

SARIKA. Experts, yes, absolutely.

ROBIN. Look around you, Sarika.

I know every inch of this hectare of land, I know the flora and fauna, the microflora and microfauna, every moss and every grub and every particle of soil I've studied through every season, every condition of weather, recorded years of data of tidal patterns, of wind directions, of sea currents,

logged patterns of bird migrations, studied the life cycles of lugworms and sandworms, and I know about cloud formation and silting, and am I an expert? I can't even say for sure what'll happen tonight.

WILL. Dad, you need to show a little bit of respect to Sarika, okay?

ROBIN. If you say so, son, if you say so.

Pause.

SARIKA. It's fine. It's stimulating.

Because I feel you are precisely the sort of person we should be working with.

For the reasons you suggest.

ROBIN. Oh, I doubt that.

SARIKA. Of course you are, Robin. You're a brilliant scientist. Scrupulous. Passionate.

JENNY. What have you been telling her, Will?

ROBIN. I don't call myself a scientist any more.

SARIKA. I work with an old colleague of yours.

WILL. Sar. I don't think –

ROBIN. I don't have any old colleagues.

SARIKA. He speaks very highly of you.

ROBIN. Must be thinking of someone else, love.

SARIKA. No, no, I don't think so. Colin Jenks?

Silence. ROBIN *looks at* WILL, *at* SARIKA, *at* JENNY.

JENNY. You know Colin?

SARIKA. Yes, of course. He's Chief Government Scientific Advisor. We work together closely.

JENNY. Yes, we see Colin from time to time.

He's been a great friend to Robin, over the years.

WILL. Oh, come on. He ripped off Dad's ideas.

ROBIN. Did I ever say that?

JENNY. He's been a staunch friend of your dad's.

ROBIN. I told him he was wrong.

SARIKA. About what?

ROBIN. I wrote and told him when he took up the post, I said we have to start doing without it all – governments, Civil Servants, politicians, democracy, all of it.

SARIKA. We can hardly do without democracy.

ROBIN. Oh, you think voting'll stop the great die-out, huh! You think a show of hands ever stopped a wave in its tracks?

WILL. Dad, this is wild talk –

JENNY. I told you your dad loves his little apocalypse.

ROBIN. Here comes the line, you'll like this, Will, this is her psychological line –

JENNY. Oh, come on, Rob, every morning, on the web, what's the melt rate in the Arctic, oh, goody, worse than we thought, I was right, I was right all along –

ROBIN. Well, yes, there will be some considerable satisfaction in being proved – in Will's work being vindicated –

WILL. What do you mean, 'in being proved'?

My work's to disprove your work.

SARIKA. Didn't Colin and you work together on the Stability Hypothesis? If I'm frank I don't particularly like Colin.

I find him a pretty frustrating proposition, very fond of his own voice.

ROBIN. Quiet!

JENNY. What is it?

ROBIN. Listen.

The sound of a bird – perhaps an egret.

There! There. Look.

He rushes to get his binoculars.

Ssh.

SARIKA. What, what is it?

ROBIN. Please keep your voice down.

JENNY. It's just the barn owl, Rob.

ROBIN (*whispers*). Look. Will.

The cry again. WILL *looks, grunts.*

What do you reckon?

WILL. Can't make it out.

ROBIN. There. White like a ghost.

WILL. Where?

ROBIN. Its plumage makes it exposed.

Non-native plumage.

WILL. I can't see it.

ROBIN. Look at it. It's sensing the change.

The up-currents. The air pressure dropping.

It knows.

SARIKA. Yes, I see something. Little egret. I've seen them. In Nigeria. Fabulous.

Silence as they think about this. JENNY *gets up and clears the plates.*

JENNY. I'll get the pudding.

WILL. Let me get that, please –

SARIKA. I'll check on the news. Can I – ?

JENNY. No, it's fine, it's fine.

JENNY goes into the house; SARIKA *wanders after.* WILL *drinks more, as does* ROBIN; WILL *stands.*

WILL. Dad. Dad. You… okay?

ROBIN. Sea's closer in.

It's all going and they're going to let it go.

WILL. Let's not talk about 'theys', Dad. 'They' are just 'us' somewhere else.

ROBIN. Let the sea claim its own.

WILL. It's swollen, isn't it?

ROBIN. The sea'll take us to the next phase.

Pause. They look at each other.

WILL. What's all this about phases, Dad?

ROBIN. No, look at you, you're jet-lagged, we'll chat in the morning.

WILL. No. I'm ready, Dad. Tell me about the sea.

ROBIN. Might take a bit of explaining.

WILL. Ready for that too.

ROBIN. Jen! Jenny!

JENNY enters, looking apprehensive, with the pudding, bowls of gooseberry.

Leave that.

JENNY. It's our first gooseberries, three weeks early this year, they like the warming.

ROBIN. We can have it later, we need the space.

JENNY. What's going on?

She looks at WILL.

Love, it's late. Let's eat our pudding –

ROBIN. Skip pudding, put the coffee on and we'll be done in half an hour. Will, help me clear up.

ROBIN goes.

WILL. Yeah. Let's do it.

WILL *goes in.*

JENNY. Oh. I could do with a fag.

SARIKA *re-enters.*

SARIKA. I have a supply.

JENNY. I don't smoke.

SARIKA. Me neither. But I always carry one or two for emergencies.

She gets one out and lights it for JENNY.

JENNY. What are you doing here?

SARIKA. I'm sorry?

JENNY. What is it that you're after?

SARIKA. Will wanted me to meet you –

JENNY. No. That's not it. You want something else.

SARIKA. Nothing sinister, I don't think.

Will's a wonderful guy.

JENNY. I'm aware of that. Thanks, for this.

Pause.

I always wanted a daughter.

SARIKA. It's a very male world here.

JENNY. You think so? I try and fill it with something approaching love.

I have felt, with Will, over the years, I have felt him slipping away from me. Blaming me for things I'd no part in.

SARIKA. Oh, he loves you very much.

You're very… close.

JENNY. You're an only child?

SARIKA. Not at all, no. One of six actually.

JENNY. Yes, this was it. We were all too close.

He didn't make many friends, we were so absorbed in our concerns.

SARIKA. You gave him a very special childhood.

JENNY. I felt I had to keep him busy, busy all the time.

SARIKA. Robin or Will?

JENNY. Oh, I need to – to sit down. Oh, I'm drunk.

SARIKA. Have more. It's okay.

JENNY. I shouldn't be saying any of this.

SARIKA. You don't have to say anything.

JENNY. Everything had to be set aside for the work.

You probably think this is just a pretty place, a refuge. It is. But it's part of something, some higher purpose.

SARIKA. I don't follow you.

JENNY. You wonder how you allow yourself to become what you become, but each step makes perfect sense. I fell for Robin. Seemed so clear. He was more alive than anyone I knew.

And Will. There's hardly any of me in him, I'm educated, okay, but I never – I could never – challenge anything, always on the outside and when Rob, when this thing, when Rob –

She looks at SARIKA.

SARIKA. Go on.

JENNY. I have fought all my life for what you see.

ROBIN *and* WILL *come on carrying something.*

ROBIN. You always say it, Will, our problem is we're ruled by people with absolutely no scientific background, it's a disgrace, the illiteracy –

WILL. It is a disgrace, I agree, but if we don't get involved – here. On the table.

ROBIN *makes space for what looks like a stage-design model box covered in a kind of protective fleece.* ROBIN *clears a space on the table.* WILL *pours himself another glass of wine.* SARIKA *gets out her BlackBerry which is now dry.* ROBIN *is manipulating a pencil torch; with great solemnity he pulls back the fleece to reveal a relief map of the reserve within a tank with markings on the side. He has a measuring vessel.*

ROBIN. Okay. Here we are. Okay.

Everyone see okay?

JENNY. What is this?

ROBIN. Just something I've been working on.

JENNY. Where – how? What is this?

ROBIN. Effectively our land in cross-section, from about two kilometres inland to about five-hundred metres out to sea.

The different habitats: salt marsh, dunes, intertidal zone, freshwater lagoon. And here's where we are. And now you see this Perspex screen here, which functions like a sort of sluice gate, on which I have marked a scale for a range of sea levels, in terms of the past and the projected future.

WILL *grunts.*

Now, water.

He reaches for a jug on the table, pours some methodically into the measuring jug.

Will, can you pour?

SARIKA. I'll do it. What exactly is being poured?

In real terms?

WILL. Water, I guess.

They laugh.

SARIKA. I mean, what does it represent?

ROBIN. Just for reference, what you have there is the amount of water that would form the equivalent to the sort of volume

we might see tonight, all things being equal, during a fierce storm. If you could pour it in up to here – stop there.

Already we can see it's theoretically higher than the marsh, up to the dunes even. Look, look closer.

WILL. Yup.

JENNY. This is tonight?

SARIKA. It looks clear out there.

ROBIN. Now we are betting on current estimates of sea level. But what if we factor in the sort of result emerging from Will's work, as and when it's concluded – if you could pour up to this level. Good.

WILL. But what does that represent?

ROBIN. I'm projecting forward to this autumn, say.

Can we say no summer ice in the Arctic?

Say a nought-point-five to one-metre sea-level rise?

SARIKA. Is that a safe extrapolation, Will?

ROBIN. Will, you can confirm the potential of a metre rise –

WILL. Could be an awful lot worse –

SARIKA. You think that?

ROBIN. We're talking about this locality, of course.

WILL. Impossible to speak in exact volumes.

ROBIN. Now pour up to the halfway mark there.

Let's imagine we got the Stability Hypothesis wrong.

Imagine we lose most of Greenland, imagine the West Antarctic Sheet itself breaks apart.

Take it up to this level. Right up, right up.

SARIKA. Well, there it's happening, your deluge.

She pours the water.

ROBIN. And because it's, let's say, a '53 event –

SARIKA. ''53 event'?

WILL. Major flood, err, hit this whole coast –

ROBIN. – particularly strong spring tide and, look, pour a little more, we have major inundation –

WILL. Yeah, Dad, but it won't come from above –

ROBIN. Okay, this is a simulation but you don't deny the premise?

WILL. Well, I am not sure exactly – but go on –

ROBIN. Grant me the premise, Will, it's consensual, it's mainstream –

WILL. Okay, fine, a major spring tide, fine –

ROBIN. This is what happens, this –

He pulls up the sluice and the water spills all over the model.

There, there, look, utter inundation of all areas under five metres over sea level which is most of here – and we have to factor in the surge –

He is splashing and moving water about with his hands.

SARIKA. The surge?

ROBIN. The wind driving the sea inland, tidal currents into land, so-called positive surge. And tides are very localised and unpredictable – look at how the so-called defences, see how they exacerbate the surge, here and here – if you resist the sea, you enrage it.

Remove them, you in effect implement Phase Four.

WILL. Phase Four of what?

ROBIN. The sea's impervious to control.

Every attempt to brook its will fails.

Every shield or defence only inflames it further. The only solution is to allow it to find its course. The lesson they took from '53 was more barriers, more dykes, more drains, more

groins when the real answer is more marsh, mass retreat inland, a whole new idea of living.

Now look, its inroads are more extensive, but the effect is less destructive. Work with the sea. Appease it, if you like.

Phase Four is the only viable plan. No plan at all.

The water has immersed the whole reserve.

How do you like it?

Pause.

SARIKA. Is that a plan or a suicide note?

JENNY. Why, why have you said nothing of this to me?

ROBIN. Of course this is premature without Will's – conclusions.

JENNY. What are the implications for us, here?

ROBIN. This site is the ultimate laboratory. Everything we have built here, all these conditions make us the model site for measuring sea-level impacts; we are a Petri dish, we are the canary in the coalmine –

WILL. You keep saying Phase Four; Phase Four of what?

ROBIN. Phase One, map the land; Phase Two, study marine impacts on flora and fauna; Phase Three, view tidal impacts through a thirty-seven-year cycle; and now this, this is Phase Four: return the land to the sea.

JENNY. But the water must be right up to the house –

WILL. You've not done anything… to the sea defences?

ROBIN. That term in itself is a misnomer.

SARIKA. It's radical, I'll give you that.

ROBIN. Phase Five is the end of human habitation altogether; marsh prevails; no caravan sites, no retirement homes, Hunstanton too will have to go, back comes the pristine landscape of the Holocene era –

Suddenly SARIKA*'s BlackBerry pings.*

Can't you turn that off?

SARIKA. Ah. It's working. Yay! I better just go –

She goes in.

WILL. Dad, this, what you've done here is, I'm sorry, this is a counsel of despair –

ROBIN. It's an act of optimism, William –

WILL. How can we abandon the coast?

The whole economy is maritime and with population densities inland –

ROBIN. But your research will show –

WILL. We're not estuarine birds, we're not lugworms. We have technology, we have resources, we have knowledge, we have structures, okay, we're not Bangladesh – this, this is the product of thirty years of your refusal to engage –

JENNY. Will, that's enough.

ROBIN *suddenly seizes* WILL.

ROBIN. Will, I'm your biggest fan, you know.

I've revelled in every step of your career.

WILL. This is not the time to, to say – to –

ROBIN. I fondly think you've done what perhaps I failed to do and I am very proud –

WILL. Dad, get off me. Please. Okay. I'm going to ask some questions. I have these questions, I need to ask these questions – now just hang on – Mum – now. Shit, I'm drunk.

Why, why did you come home early?

In 1973?

JENNY. He didn't, he came home –

ROBIN. What's this about? This is irrelevant.

WILL. You go with Colin, for three winters you go.

You establish the Stability Hypothesis. Now, is this right?

ROBIN. The work we did underpinned the Hypothesis.

WILL. He didn't come back till '74, but you, you came back earlier, didn't you?

ROBIN. Let's talk about the future –

WILL. Don't confuse me, don't –

You broke off your work? In '73?

JENNY. Yes. Okay, yes, you're right, he came back.

ROBIN. Jenny!

JENNY. You know you did, it doesn't matter –

WILL. But why?

ROBIN. I was – okay, I became unwell.

WILL. No, no, come on, what do you mean, 'unwell'?

JENNY. Yes. He was unwell, Will.

WILL. What you found did something to you, right, Dad? You found something out and –

SARIKA (*off*). Will! I need to talk to you.

WILL. Hang on, please, I'm busy here, love.

Pause.

ROBIN. There's more to ask?

WILL. Oh, we haven't even started.

ROBIN. I see.

WILL. What did you find out, Dad? That made you so sick?

Pause.

ROBIN. I'll talk alone or not at all.

JENNY. What?

WILL. It's only family.

ROBIN. No. Alone.

JENNY. You won't achieve anything worth doing here and
    you'll cause a lot of –

ROBIN. I can't do this with her here.

JENNY. 'Her'?

WILL. Mum. Please.

JENNY. I always said there was nothing to hide, nothing to be
    ashamed of.

WILL. Mum.

JENNY. We were protecting you as good parents –

WILL. Mum!

    JENNY *goes. Pause.*

ROBIN. The data made no sense.

    Generally across the ice sheet it conformed to type. But at
    Pine Island – the ice was streaming off, yes, we were both
    shocked by the warming of the sea, the melt.

    Because we didn't come looking for it, we assumed the exact
    opposite –

    It made no sense at all.

    In some sections it was losing more ice than it was gaining.

WILL. Even then?

ROBIN. So, okay, Colin said it had to make sense, and the only
    way it could was that what we found was localised,
    regionalised – but what if we were to generalise, I said?
    Long long arguments about causes, attribution; what caused
    the warming? El Niño? Sunspots?

    Ozone depletion? Natural warming. Had no conception
    about CO_2. And why so fast, you know. You, you know the
    complexity – we didn't have the gear, the computers, the ice-
    core records. What if Pine Island was in fact typical, what if
    the ice sheet was dynamic not stable? Colin was adamant –
    this data was unusable and were I to use it, he would – it
    would make an utter fool out of us, both of us. We were in

our tent, in the middle of a storm, we actually fought, physically, ha! He struck camp. Compelled me to go further inland.

Pursued his own measurements. All credit to him, he found what he needed.

WILL. Jesus.

Pause. JENNY *reapproaches.*

ROBIN. But I couldn't stop thinking about that warming, doing the maths, if this much heat generated this much ice loss, generating ocean warming, more ice loss, reduced reflectivity, more warming, more heat, more ice loss, sea-level rise, more ice loss, more heat, more ice loss, more sea, less albedo, more heat –

JENNY. Stop, stop, you made yourself ill then you're –

WILL. What, what did Colin do?

JENNY. Colin knew it was dangerous, he advised you –

ROBIN. He was on the verge of a massive breakthrough and what I thought made no sense, couldn't compute, I mean, how were we to explain an effect with no discernible cause, an effect where any conceivable cause made no sense, but he got the data he needed to –

WILL. He distorted the data?

ROBIN. To be fair, only in regard to Pine Island.

There it was adjusted… down.

To achieve… consistency.

WILL. You should have published what you found.

ROBIN. Publish some anomalous figures from an isolated glacier that I couldn't explain?

Undermine the most robust hypothesis in modern glaciology?

WILL. You, you knew the ice sheet was melting and you suppressed it!

And what was I supposed to be, some sort of, what, some sort of proxy for you, supposed to do the job you failed to do, right, all these years, the two of you, all these years and you, you knew what was coming, but you, what, you sat on your hands?

ROBIN *sits heavily and buries his face in his hands.*

JENNY. That's a disgraceful thing to say.

SARIKA *comes on.*

SARIKA. Will! Please. It's urgent. Something's happened.

WILL. In a minute.

SARIKA. I mean, serious –

WILL. Yes, yes, I'll come but can you just – ?

She takes him in, then goes back inside.

JENNY. He tried his best. To make it more widely known.

ROBIN. No, Jenny.

JENNY. No, it's only fair.

WILL. It was you, wasn't it?

ROBIN. What?

WILL. What was your plan?

ROBIN. What?

WILL. What was your plan?

ROBIN. What plan?

WILL. This.

He pulls out the photocopied document.

JENNY. What's this?

ROBIN'*s staring at the paper.*

ROBIN. They promised there'd be no record.

JENNY. You said that, you said they –

ROBIN. Promised no record, off the –

WILL. What did you discuss?

JENNY. Where on earth did you get this?

ROBIN. I don't bloody believe this.

JENNY. Have you been – ?

WILL. What did you discuss?

ROBIN. They weren't ready to hear about it. Coastal retreat, worldwide coastal retreat? The exit from the oil economy? Oh dear.

Phasing out cars, phasing out consumption, reverse road building, creating self-sufficiency?

Can you imagine writing it down, going like a lamb to them, Colin rightly, rightly putting me right on whatever occasion he could, why would he not, got to distance yourself from lunacy like that, right, right –

SARIKA *comes on; she has her bag, her coat on.*

SARIKA. Will – I'm sorry. I am sorry. This is not the time but – I have to get to London – there's been some event, some –

JENNY. What is this?

SARIKA. Utter, freak flooding in the west –

WILL. A flood? Tidal?

SARIKA. Probably – I only know there's fatalities, that it's apparently, err, some huge tidal event, far larger than anyone presumed, they obviously really fucked up the predictive stuff, happened very fast, hit the outskirts of Bristol to, to devastating effect.

Sorry – I know this is – look – sorry –

Pause.

WILL. Jesus.

JENNY. A what – a flood?

SARIKA *nods.*

ROBIN. It's starting.

Silence.

SARIKA. And it's just, it'll be just hitting the news.

I mean, this is awful but – okay – this is the best thing that could have happened. We've all been recalled, and I think – I know – this is the time.

WILL. Right. Okay.

Silence.

JENNY. The time for what?

SARIKA. So, look, I took the liberty of calling a cab and they're gonna meet us up on the Lynn road and they reckon that should get us to the last King's Cross train, but if not, we're authorised to take it all the way.

JENNY. What are you doing?

WILL. What am I doing?

SARIKA. I can explain – if Will hasn't –

ROBIN. Let's hear it from him.

WILL. Okay, Dad. Okay.

I am going into Government.

SARIKA. We want –

ROBIN. Be quiet, you!

WILL. Now you don't – yes, yes, I am going into Government, I'm going to smash the Stability Hypothesis.

SARIKA. Will's going to play a major role –

ROBIN. I asked you to be quiet!

JENNY. Rob –

WILL. Don't you talk to her like that –

ROBIN. You came back for that?

WILL. You're in no place to dictate what I do.

ROBIN. Broke off your research for that?

WILL. I asked for a sabbatical. And do you know what they said? They said was that for personal reasons, I said no, they said was I experiencing psychological problems, I said in a way, they said like your father –

JENNY. Now you're being cruel.

SARIKA. We don't have time for this, truly.

I'll head off and try to –

WILL. Yeah. Yeah, you – yeah.

SARIKA *goes*.

You taught me contempt for anything but data! Okay. But what is a fact on its own, Dad? It's nothing. I mean, isn't science about making the world better?

Isn't that what you tried to do back then, Dad?

ROBIN. Science is about telling the truth and no more.

WILL. Well, you're a fine model for that.

ROBIN. How could you give up your work for her?

WILL. This, this'll be my work now.

And I am taking my work, taking it to the highest level –

ROBIN. Oh, and you think that'll somehow, what, change things – to throw in your lot with the liars and fools who have got us into this mess – to –

WILL. If your work had emerged in 1974 –

ROBIN. My work did emerge, boy.

And they spat in my face.

I made the mistake of thinking the truth was its own ambassador. And if you do this, now, you will make the exact same mistake again. These people, they use you, this girl will use you too, suck you dry, suck the good out of you, make you nothing but a pimp to power –

WILL hits ROBIN *in the face.*

WILL. Shit. Dad. I didn't –

JENNY. You hurt him. What are you doing – Rob?

She goes to him.

WILL. Shit – is he – Dad – is he all right?

JENNY. Rob – he's very – frail – I told you – I told you that – why did you hit him?

WILL. I didn't – shit –

Car horn off.

I'm sorry. Dad.

He goes to him; ROBIN *waves him away.*

ROBIN. Off you go – chop, chop.

WILL. You were wrong back then, and now, you're absolutely wrong again.

ROBIN. Go and tell that to Colin. Go and tell that to your new paymasters.

WILL. I'm sorry for –

I really am sorry. But I have to do this. Mum.

WILL tries to hold her; she flinches away.

Dad.

ROBIN *sits down and fiddles with his model.*

I don't fucking believe this.

Car horn off.

I don't –

He goes. Silence. The car drives off. ROBIN *and* JENNY *stand.*

ROBIN. We didn't eat the fruit, did we?

JENNY. No. We didn't eat the fruit.

Blackout.

ACT TWO

Scene One

Norfolk, September. As before, a table is laid with tablecloth, but now places are set for two; as before, the hurricane lamp. We sense a quickening of the wind and the sea is louder than before. ROBIN sits with binoculars. Suddenly the cry of an egret.

ROBIN. Where are you now?

He scans around with his binoculars.

Pretty beggar. Preening yourself now?

No, you ought to clear off, clear out of here.

This is gonna catch you napping, southerner. This ain't the Rance here! Not the Bay of Biscay! That's the North Sea there. The German Ocean. Cold sea. This is Northern Europe. This not your latitude.

The beating of wings, somewhere.

That's it, that's the way, fuck off, fuck back off to France or Spain, good girl.

JENNY *walks on with dinner.*

JENNY. It can't hear you.

ROBIN. No.

JENNY. Nor can it comprehend you.

ROBIN. No.

JENNY. And swearing at birds is a sure sign of early-onset dementia.

He laughs.

Okay, here we are.

Sea bass. In sea salt. On a bed of our parsley.

My spuds.

ROBIN. My word, look at that.

Ah, not the lovely 'Nicola' spuds?

JENNY. Yes, the lovely Nicola.

ROBIN. Creamy, yet firm Nicola.

JENNY. Don't be creepy, Rob, it's a potato.

But I think you'll find the *coup de grâce* is sea-kale, fried in garlic with pine nuts and a splash of lemon.

ROBIN. Anything to mask the bitterness.

Shall I be Ainsley?

JENNY. You be Ainsley, yes.

He tastes it, plays up the whole TV-chef thing.

ROBIN. So the astringent, even sour taste of the sea-kale, its native rough-hewn texture is offset brilliantly by the acetic acid of the lemon and then, in a masterstroke, further neutralised by the tang of garlic until in effect, the entire taste of the sea-kale has been – obliterated.

JENNY. You bugger, it has a lovely taste.

ROBIN. It does, it does.

JENNY. Tastes of here.

She sits. They start to eat.

ROBIN. Yeah. Yes, it does.

It's fabulous. It's fabulous.

JENNY. Mmm.

ROBIN. Those spuds are – God!

JENNY. They just love that soil. Thrive in it.

ROBIN. It's the mix of salt and wind-blown earth –

JENNY. And I think it's all the bird dung actually.

ROBIN. And that kale. Now, I did that kale a disservice.

JENNY. I did debone the fish but watch out for any – remnants, any –

The telephone rings in the house.

Shall we ignore that?

ROBIN. Let it go to message.

JENNY. Yes.

Pause. It rings. ROBIN eats, JENNY stops.

I suppose we should at least update him.

ROBIN. On what?

JENNY. Nothing, no.

Pause. It rings.

ROBIN. Wouldn't want to distract him from his numerous duties.

JENNY. No. That would be wrong.

Pause. We hear a message being left, inaudible. JENNY picks at her food.

JENNY. Funnily enough, I saw him on the news.

ROBIN. Why were you watching the news?

JENNY. I happened to put it on.

And he came across well. No. Tetchy.

Impatient.

ROBIN. I expect the questions were moronic.

JENNY. Actually he came across well at first.

He was the only one who seemed to know what they were talking about. Wearing a suit too.

I've only seen him in a suit once, when he wore your old DJ, when he graduated.

Do you remember? Far too small. I had to let down the sleeves. He insisted on this clip-on dickie bow. But here, he had a new suit, I bet she chose it for him.

ROBIN. Probably some advisor.

JENNY. He hadn't properly brushed his hair.

He looked like he does when he's just woken up.

He never considers his hair. Like a child.

ROBIN. That sort of thing goes down well. With the media. Comical hair. Mad scientists.

JENNY. Yet, my God, he was clear. Authoritative.

ROBIN. That's the problem, isn't it.

JENNY. Mmm. What? Why's that a problem?

ROBIN. He's there to make things plausible.

JENNY. Isn't it good to have him in there, it must be good?

ROBIN. We're not discussing this, Jenny.

JENNY. I suppose a part of me just thinks that must be good.

ROBIN. He should be doing science, not speaking for 'science'. You never see politicians these days. Only scientists speaking for them, cleaning up after them.

JENNY. There was a lot of confusion about tonight. About how bad tonight could be.

ROBIN. They have not the faintest idea what will happen tonight.

Pause.

JENNY. We're not talking about this.

ROBIN. No, we're not.

JENNY. My fault. I brought it up.

ROBIN. Yes. Eat your gorgeous meal.

JENNY. Yes.

Pause. She stops eating and toys with the food.

So where's it reached now?

ROBIN. Oh. I don't know. Spurn Head, I expect.

JENNY. So that's...?

ROBIN. An hour away, maybe.

JENNY. An hour! Only an hour. And yet it feels – still.

ROBIN. The wind's quickening. Look at the sea. Getting more turbulent. And there, look at the cloud banks to the north.

JENNY. Those are angry clouds.

I love that effect. The sun, backlighting them.

They stand out, in relief.

ROBIN. Yes, very pretty.

JENNY. Will kept talking about surges.

ROBIN. There. What would he know about that?

Is he an oceanologist? Generalising, creating pointless ignorant panic?

JENNY. He got rather plaintive trying to explain it.

Poor lamb. You know how he blushes, when he's angry, like you, as if you find it impossible to imagine that what you're saying could be misunderstood.

ROBIN. Look, tonight's about here, right? Thirty-seven years. It's about building dams, clearing ground, it's about all of that.

JENNY. Yes.

ROBIN. Thirty-seven years of love and work.

JENNY. Yes.

ROBIN. A ruined watchhouse, a hectare of wetland, you and me both. Without us, what would be here?

JENNY. A row of holiday homes and a hideous sea wall.

Pause.

ROBIN. Ah. You know what.

I forgot to open this. Bugger.

He pulls a bottle of wine from a bucket.

Been saving it for a rainy day.

JENNY. I think this'll pass for that, love.

He opens it expertly. Pours her a glass. She drinks, coughs, spits it out.

What is this?

He pats her back. Drinks it himself.

ROBIN. Elderflower wine.

Vin '74. Smelt of hay, looked like urine.

JENNY. Where did you find that? It's disgusting.

ROBIN. Still good… to taste. Kept it.

JENNY. It's gone off. Pour it away.

Robin. You idiot. Could be toxic.

ROBIN. I think it's matured nicely.

JENNY. It's full of rot and sediment. Urghh!

She drinks water. Laughs.

You idiot!

Fared better than your Norfolk ale, anyway.

ROBIN. Oh yes, the Norfolk ale!

JENNY. The reek of it, of the malt.

ROBIN. Oh, and that summer of the gas build-up, the bloody – fermentation –

JENNY. Oh God, yes, you, you running around with these –

ROBIN. – exploding bloody –

JENNY. – ice-cream soda bottles of –

ROBIN. – foaming out like –

JENNY. – the sight of you –

ROBIN. – Will, screaming at me!

They laugh.

JENNY. And what, what did it taste like?

ROBIN. Sour tea, sour bloody tea!

JENNY. And it left such a stain on your teeth.

ROBIN. Okay, it was an abortive… experiment.

God, yeah.

Pause.

JENNY. And I look back on those days, I dunno, with incredible fondness.

ROBIN. Do you?

JENNY. Of course I do.

ROBIN. I sort of thought I'd forced you into –

JENNY. Nobody forces me into anything.

Did I ever suggest that?

ROBIN. You would have been justified…

JENNY. I made it my life, didn't I? Didn't I?

ROBIN. Yeah. Yes, you absolutely did. And I thank you for it, Jenny.

JENNY. Working all day and then sleeping so deeply.

ROBIN. You know I didn't believe in it. That it would work.

JENNY. Oh, he tells me that now.

ROBIN. Truly I didn't. Not until the birds came.

When the birds came, then I knew it would be okay.

JENNY. Those harriers, yes, the marsh, the marsh harrier.

That hen harrier even – they loved that dead ash tree, I was all for felling it, you said let it stand, and they loved it, that ash tree.

It was a sort of benediction, their choosing us.

ROBIN. No, no religious stuff, we simply got the conditions right.

JENNY. Isn't it a miracle, them finding our hectare out of all that land, choosing us?

ROBIN. Just so little left elsewhere, the freshwater lagoon, the salt marsh, the dunes, the habitat.

Give them an inch and they take it. I mean, where'll they go now?

No. Sorry.

Suddenly a siren calls, off. They stop eating for a moment.

ROBIN. I don't see what purpose that serves.

JENNY. No.

Pause.

Presumably they don't sound it for fun.

ROBIN. It's just procedure.

Don't want to get sued if anyone gets the slightest bit wet.

JENNY. I've never heard it before.

ROBIN. It signifies panic and we're not going to panic.

JENNY. Yes. They're just covering themselves.

ROBIN. If they were serious there would be helicopters, house-to-house evacuations.

JENNY. Will said there would be, there would be evacuations.

ROBIN. It's a matter of individual discretion.

JENNY. Right.

Look, you can see, hardly a breeze.

Must be some way off.

ROBIN. The irony of this whole thing is the reaction is worse than the problem.

JENNY. Yes. Yes. Frightening people out of their houses. On a weekend.

ROBIN. Exactly.

JENNY. Must be a field day for, say, burglars.

ROBIN. Of course.

The siren again.

Now that is fatuous.

JENNY. Oh, he claimed it would exceed 1953. Will.

ROBIN. No chance.

JENNY. Because, he said rising sea levels would make it more lethal.

ROBIN. This is the whole thing. They want authoritative statements and you are compelled and you can't blame Will for this, you are compelled to give these closed answers, do you discuss probability, no, risk, no and then you end up looking a fool. Abusing your position.

JENNY. Yes.

ROBIN. Disgracing yourself.

JENNY. Yes.

Pause.

Scared the birds too, look.

ROBIN. Yes, yes, it has, look at them, look at the –

The sound of hundreds of drumming wing-beats as a huge flock of geese alights and circles; it's incredibly loud.

Oh God. The Canada geese!

JENNY. My God. Must be two hundred!

ROBIN. Must be at least two hundred! The noise!

JENNY. I didn't know we had so – ! Wow!

ROBIN. Look, the lapwings too, look!

JENNY. Even the lapwings!

ROBIN. And the martins! The teal!

JENNY. Must be five-hundred-odd birds!

ROBIN. And there, the oystercatchers too –

JENNY. Off, off –

ROBIN. Off again, off.

Weeks early.

JENNY. Swallows gone, martins gone.

ROBIN. Even the avocets've –

Pause. The sound fades away.

ROBIN *is tearful; he returns to his meal. Eats on.*

JENNY *stands.*

Finish it. It'll grow cold.

JENNY. Mmm.

ROBIN. As you put so much effort in. Finish it.

JENNY. Never heard it so quiet.

ROBIN. Oh, where did you get the sea bass?

From Cley? Such a clean taste.

The wine too. Jenny. Finish it. Please.

She sits down, toys with the food.

JENNY. Not a car on the road.

ROBIN. How it should be. Quiet.

JENNY. Why's the coast so dark?

ROBIN. No traffic noise, no light pollution.

They should do this more often.

JENNY. No, look, no lights to the west.

ROBIN. You should be delighted. Talk about 'cut your carbon'.

Are you really not going to finish that?

She shakes her head.

Well, that's a terrible… waste.

He moves her plate across, eats for her.

Ah, you let it go cold.

JENNY. What?

ROBIN. What a bloody waste. Really.

JENNY. Sorry. I'm sorry. Sorry.

There's more in –

ROBIN. No. No, I'm fine. Fine.

Pause. A more muted siren now from further down the coast.

JENNY. Is that Lynn now?

ROBIN *nods his head.*

Don't they evacuate? Or check?

They probably assume we're not here.

How would they know?

Aren't they meant to do a house-to-house?

ROBIN. Doubt they'll bother with us.

JENNY. But what'll we do if they come?

ROBIN. No, they won't.

JENNY. What do you mean?

ROBIN. I mean, I just mean they can't.

JENNY. Of course they can if they want to.

Why can't they?

ROBIN. Well.

JENNY. Rob? Why couldn't they come? Robin.

Robin! Why can't they come?

ROBIN. Well. Because I blocked the road.

   The approach road.

   Pause.

JENNY. What? You – what? How?

ROBIN. Towed the old boat up. On the trailer.

   Laid it across.

JENNY. You blocked the approach road?

ROBIN. They could walk past it, of course.

   Just not offering any encouragement.

   Not that they'll come anyway.

JENNY. Okay. Why, why did you do that, Rob?

   What if we wanted to – drive, say?

ROBIN. Where, where would we drive to, where?

JENNY. Sorry, you blocked the approach road?

ROBIN. You're repeating yourself. We've nowhere worth
   going. We've got no good reason to go.

   We don't want them coming and intervening.

   Shifting us somewhere that means nothing to us.

   No. We'll be fine here.

JENNY. The defences will protect us.

ROBIN. Well, they are, as I've often said, part of the problem.
   Be fascinating to see how the sea behaves without obstacles
   like that.

JENNY. Without the defences?

ROBIN. Mmm.

JENNY. Why would we be without the defences?

ROBIN. I breached them. Well, I, you know, I let them fall into
   disrepair. The groins were pretty rotten anyway. More benign
   neglect. Because actually in April they held up.

So that night proved inconclusive.

JENNY. In what respect?

ROBIN. Oh, you know. In terms of the plan.

Pause.

JENNY. What are we doing?

ROBIN. You know what we're doing.

JENNY. I don't, no, Rob, I don't think I do.

I mean, what are we really doing?

Answer me. Truly.

Pause.

I mean, have you lied to me about tonight?

ROBIN. No. Nothing is sure, of course.

JENNY. You're sure.

ROBIN. How could I be? Am I an oceanologist?

I've the barest knowledge of tidal action. Incredibly basic.
And I'm no meteorologist.

These things, to understand them, you need such powerful
models, you need satellite tracking, they generally get it wrong.

JENNY. But if they haven't, what are we doing?

ROBIN. Sticking it out. Seeing it out.

We're sticking it out.

Finishing our supper.

Drinking a bottle of wine.

Seeing it through, love.

It's fine, absolutely – just go over the plan.

JENNY. What?

ROBIN. Just repeat the procedures we agreed. Jenny.

She sits.

JENNY. Yes. Yes. Okay. Everything is moved upstairs.

ROBIN. Yes. And?

JENNY. Turned off the gas, electricity, water –

ROBIN. Paperwork?

JENNY. Yep. Got the insurance documents on me –

ROBIN. All items of personal, all treasured items –

JENNY. Packed our bags with a change of clothes –

ROBIN. Put plugs in the sinks –

JENNY. – the bath –

ROBIN. Plugged the water inlet pipes with towels –

JENNY. Disconnected the washing machine –

ROBIN. Bottles of fresh water, torch, first-aid kit, tinned food –
   yes. Yes?

JENNY. Yes.

   Pause.

ROBIN. So it's fine, right?

JENNY. Yes.

ROBIN. So, let's eat our pudding, shall we?

JENNY. Yes.

   The phone rings in the house.

ROBIN. We should disconnect that bloody –

JENNY. I'll –

ROBIN. No, it's fine. Let me go and –

JENNY. Perhaps, Rob, perhaps we should stay in touch.

ROBIN. With who exactly?

   ROBIN's *gone in.* JENNY, *alone, pulls out her mobile. She
   calls, watching the house at all times. She can't get through.*

TILL 1
NATIONAL THEATRE BOOKSHOP
SOUTH BANK
LONDON SE1 9PX
T: 020 7452 3456
BOOKSHOP@NATIONALTHEATRE.ORG.U

DATE:11/05/2009   TIME:19:03

REFERENCE: TIL19940

SALE

ICC
VISA
**** **** **** 3351
AID: A0000000031010
EXPIRY: 03/11
PAN SEQ NO: 02
AUTH CODE:138862   00

TOTAL SALE

GBP £9.99

PLEASE DEBIT MY ACCOUNT
CARDHOLDER PIN VERIFIED

MID:540436503318891 TID:03134161

PLEASE RETAIN THIS COPY
THIS IS NOT A VAT RECEIPT

National Theatre Bookshop
Upper Ground, South Bank,
London SE1 9PX

Telephone: 020 7452 3456
Fax: 020 7452 3457
E mail: bookshop@nationaltheatre.org.uk
website/secure online ordering:
www.nationaltheatre.org.uk/bookshop

Qty	Title	Price( )
1	9781848420526 The Continge ..	9.99

Total 9.99
Due 9.99

Payment : Credit/Debit Card 9.99
Change 0.00

19:03:17 11 May 2009
2/11111 002/0290528

VAT No. 548 1804 33

National Theatre Bookshop
Upper Ground, South Bank,
London SE1 9PX

Telephone: 020 7452 3456
Fax: 020 7452 3457
E mail: bookshop@nationaltheatre.org.uk
Website/secure online ordering:
www.nationaltheatre.org.uk/bookshop

Qty	Title		Price( )
1	9781848420526	The Continge..	9.99

Total   9.99
Due   9.99

Payment : Credit/Debit Card   9.99
Change   0.00

19:03:17 11 May 2009
2/Till1 002/0290526

VAT No. 548 1804 33

JENNY. Oh, fuck it. Fuck it. How do you…?

   She tries to text.

   Hang on, where's her…? Okay – good – oh no, not that –

   'Change message'? Yes, yes. Okay.

   Hang on. Err. S-E-A – err – R-O-B –

   She fumbles away.

   No, not that, no – where's – 'Delete'?

   Hang on. This is – 'N-O' – no, 'SEA ROB NO'? No, no.

   ROBIN *re-enters.*

ROBIN. What have you got there?

JENNY. Oh, Rob. Course, you never saw this.

ROBIN. How did you come by that phone?

JENNY. And then I could just inform him, I have been thinking, regardless of tonight, whatever happens tonight, I was thinking we should, that we have been very hasty, and I blame myself, I am a large part of that –

   ROBIN *seizes the phone.*

   Rob, don't – I'm sending –

ROBIN. You don't need that, love.

JENNY. Rob, give us that –

   She takes it back and sends the message; he snatches it back.

   – that's my phone.

ROBIN. You don't need it.

JENNY. Robin, really this is bloody stupid.

ROBIN. No, no, love. What's this? Okay.

   ROBIN *starts to dismantle it.*

   The SIM card, is it?

JENNY. I just wanted it in case of –

ROBIN. Get that case off. They have tin in them, don't they? Paradium?

JENNY. What are you doing to it?

ROBIN. Can break that down. Break it down into its components. So shoddy, look at it, where's it from? China? Look.

It's cheapjack shit, isn't it. Jenny – where will this go to die? Tin. Gold on the PCB. Plastics.

He places the disassembled phone on the table.

Could probably make use of that SIM card.

JENNY. I'll call from the house then, fine.

He shows her the cord from the telephone.

ROBIN. I was finding that distracting.

JENNY. Rob!

ROBIN. What we need to remember is we did this alone. That we are entirely alone.

Being alone is actually our strength.

If we can prevail alone we will be stronger.

Sorry, love.

Pause.

JENNY. I see. Could we, could we not at least let him know what we're doing?

ROBIN. What's he going to do? What's he going to do about it? What could he even do?

What'll you say to him?

JENNY. Well, could we not at least say we may have been right but that he's our son, he remains our son? Or maybe say that, okay, let's try again, bring her over, Sarika, yes, we perhaps misjudged her, yes, even that, she loves him, she saw things

in him, and that we acknowledge he's my only, our only son
– oh, what are we doing to ourselves here?

Pause.

ROBIN. I don't think we ate our pudding, did we?

Pause.

JENNY. Okay, I will walk up the approach road and if you have
any sense, any modicum of sense –

ROBIN. You're frightened, Jenny.

JENNY. Yes, Rob, yes I am, yes I am frightened, yes.

ROBIN. Why?

JENNY. Err, why? Well.

It's the sea, Rob. Yes. I don't, I just don't recognise it.

ROBIN. It's just a little swollen.

JENNY. No, I don't recognise it. Fine. It doesn't recognise me.

I mean, anyway, human beings can move, right. We are not
trees. We've choices in the matter. We've a duty to make a
choice, have we not?

Ah, look. The lights are gone in the – down the east coast.
Everywhere.

ROBIN. I'll bet they power down at Sizewell.

JENNY. Right.

ROBIN. Ah. Listen to that quiet.

When was it last as quiet as that?

I can hear insects ticking, the movement of marram grass, I
can hear the current sucking…

No, I didn't ever lie to you, Jenny. Told you a partial truth,
maybe.

I mean, leaving this?

Can't be done.

Be like a fish trying to swim in air, yeah?

This, this is our habitat, Jen. How could we live outside our element, tell me that?

She approaches him.

JENNY. Robin, let's walk up the lane, go up the ridge.

Robin, you've got another thirty good years in you. You don't believe in fate, do you?

Robin. So this is a natural thing. You're right.

Letting go. Retreat. Think how this has changed, the coast moving, retreating and advancing, think of it. It's no defeat to walk away from that, is it, love? It's no defeat to admit the past's mistakes, to give way to love, that's being human, isn't it, doing that?

ROBIN. You go. Yeah. You just go.

JENNY. Come with me.

ROBIN. I'm fine.

JENNY. Come with me.

ROBIN. No, I'm good here, snug here.

Ringside seat. Seriously.

You're right.

Been gearing up for this for thirty-seven years. You're right.

Relish the idea, in a way. The Hypothesis confirmed. Okay.

You don't always get to see the blow land, do you. This, this is the result, this is the data, no more models, no more predictions, this, this is the data.

Seriously, I feel contemplative. 'Cos I recognise that sea. Been dreaming of that sea for years, seeing it as I wake, tasting the salt in my mouth. And this is not the end.

You know that. I know that. Might be the end of us, what we do, but who are we?

We are the world's sickness, we are an infection, we are a disturbance in the sleep of the world and we're gonna be brushed away, sweated out.

The sea rises, the land goes, the cities go, the people are gone.

You can't fight that.

Right now, I feel alive like I haven't in – decades.

Pause.

JENNY. You know what I have started to hate?

I have started to hate science. So much.

Because I think science is a sort of madness.

Science, yes, is human madness.

You know I have made an idol of your science.

Pause.

ROBIN. Off you go then.

JENNY. I'm going to. Soon.

Pause.

ROBIN. It's just a storm.

JENNY. In the end.

ROBIN. It'll make a breach. We'll probably lose the ground floor. We'll lose the fresh water.

JENNY. It's just weather.

ROBIN. An extreme weather event.

JENNY. Yeah.

ROBIN. I'll move upstairs.

There's always been too much room, too much space heated. Too many lights.

Move into his room.

Did you roll up the carpets?

She nods.

Let the sea claim some, not all.

Keep the ash tree. The dead ash tree.

Repaint the weather boarding.

It was sea before and land before that.

When you think in continental time.

Geological time.

That's the way I'm starting to think we should think.

JENNY *stands in an agony of indecision.'On the Beach' starts to play.*

JENNY. Okay, Rob, okay.

ROBIN *gets up and holds her; she stays standing, limp.*

Blackout.

The End.

RESILIENCE

*'There are many injustices in this world,
but there is one that is never mentioned, that of climate.'*

Albert Camus

Characters

CHRISTOPHER CASSON, *Minister for Climate Change,
    forty-four*
COLIN JENKS, *Chief Government Scientific Advisor,
    sixty-seven*
TESSA FORTNUM, *Minister for Resilience, fifty-five*
WILL PAXTON, *a glaciologist, thirty-seven*
SARIKA CHATTERJEE, *a senior Civil Servant, thirty-three*

Note

*Tessa and Jenks are played by the same actors who played
Jenny and Robin in* On the Beach.

Setting

ACT ONE
A room in Whitehall; April, Sunday 9 a.m.

ACT TWO
The same; September, Saturday 8 p.m.

Time

The near future

*This text went to press before the end of rehearsals and so may
differ slightly from the play as performed.*

ACT ONE

Scene One

A cabinet room in Whitehall, Sunday 9 a.m., April. A long table with sabre-backed upholstered chairs around its dark wood; on the side wall we sense a bank of windows facing out onto Horse Guards Parade and St James's Park. On the table are a series of telephones. The main entrance is upstage leading out to a long corridor; the room is removed from the street and could almost be in a country house.

We hear Big Ben toll 9 a.m. There's an odd lack of traffic noise and the room is dim from insistent rain outside. TESSA is already present, working on her laptop; she pours herself a drink from a flask.

JENKS enters, soaked, with a Brompton bike, in luminous cycle helmet with a halogen lamp mounted on it, still flashing; he takes off a sodden cape, bike clips, leggings and lays them all out over the backs of the chairs.

Then he towels down and retrieves a soggy donner kebab from his pannier and eats it noisily, all the while still in his helmet.

JENKS. Morning.

TESSA. Morning. Late breakfast?

JENKS. Oh. Yes. Sorry. For any... aroma.

TESSA. Tends to linger.

JENKS. Yes, it does tend to. I'll... open one of these –

Goes to a window.

TESSA. They're sealed.

Bomb-proof.

JENKS. This place is becoming entirely impenetrable.

Swipe cards, sealed doors, corridors of unlabelled offices. Practically strip-searched in reception.

TESSA. I imagine they were concerned about the bike.

JENKS. They were not at all happy about the bike.

The very same people who used to wave me in, smiling, barely acknowledging me.

Are we in bloody Basra?

TESSA. Security has its own logic.

JENKS. Took me almost as long to find this room as it did to get to Millbank.

TESSA. You didn't cycle all the way from Cambridge?

JENKS laughs too loudly.

JENKS. Not quite, no, not quite. Not now. God.

No, always do the right thing: public transport – which on Sunday's invariably a replacement bus to Stevenage and a train failure in Finsbury – sorry, how did you know I'm from...?

TESSA. You're still... illuminated.

JENKS. I'm sorry?

She indicates the light on his helmet. He takes it off.

Ah. Right.

Still, good to observe the, err, precautionary principle.

TESSA. Well, it's biblically foul out there.

JENKS. No, no, a moderately heavy rainfall event.

Pause. TESSA tops up her drink.

Now that's a rather more wholesome aroma.

TESSA. Norfolk punch. Have some.

JENKS. Oh. Too early in the day.

TESSA. Non-alcoholic.

JENKS. Think it'll complement the 'donner'?

TESSA. Might offset it. Good and warming.

JENKS. Yes, it is bloody parky in here.

TESSA. Heating's set to the rhythms of governance. Off from April to October. On from November to March.

JENKS. You know what, I'll try some.

She pours him some Norfolk punch.

This is number five for me.

Came in on the back end of Morley, then, Miliband One, then Benn, then Miliband Two – now? Yes, fifth minister.

He drinks.

Mmm, that's really good, isn't it?

TESSA. The Cistercians swore by it.

JENKS. I'm sorry?

TESSA. The Cistercians, monastic order, early middle ages. You don't know Christopher?

JENKS. Casson? We've met, of course. He always seems to be in a hurry. I found him congenial. Bit of an unknown quantity, perhaps.

TESSA. As are we all.

JENKS. Oh, I'm a pretty known quantity myself.

Frankly, it all seemed in safe hands until last night; now everything feels rather hysterical. New ministry structures, parachuting in this harpy from the Home Office. Don't you think?

TESSA. I don't, no.

Nor do I think it appropriate for scientific advisors to express political opinions.

JENKS. What?

You're Civil Service, presumably?

TESSA. No. No, I'm not Civil Service, no.

We had social scientists during my time at the Home Office but isn't a 'social scientist' an oxymoron?

JENKS. Sorry, you were in the Home Office?

TESSA. You, however, seem to be the real thing.

JENKS. I don't know about 'seem'.

TESSA. Do you find the indefinition difficult? The indefinition of the role.

JENKS. Oh, my role's clearly defined. I'm here to stand outside.

TESSA. Being outside and inside must get pretty difficult. I would have thought.

JENKS. Sorry, are you sure you're not Civil Service?

TESSA. You really ought to check your briefing papers.

JENKS. I'm assiduous with my briefing papers.

TESSA. Then given that you know that as of 6 a.m. this morning there are two ministers in this department, it might have occurred to you that one of them could be me.

Pause.

JENKS. Tessa Fortnum! How stupid of me, stupid – Tessa Fortnum, Minister for Resilience, of course, Tessa, sorry.

TESSA. Very familiar all of a sudden. Colin.

JENKS. I can be incredibly… unobservant.

My wife gets utterly exasperated with me. I can be introduced to someone, get their name, have quite a conversation with them, and I – in minutes, I – good, good to meet you.

No, there's really no great mystery about my role. You get to pick my brains. Rusty though they are. Because I'm not in any way partisan, well, not politically partisan. I see myself as the nation's family doctor. I mean, you'd hardly concern yourself with your GP's voting record.

TESSA. Oh, I don't know.

JENKS. True, it's probably fair to say you guys are hardly natural bedfellows with science, from the past, given some of the tendencies, the rhetoric, but look, say, at Gummer –

TESSA. John.

JENKS. John, indeed, yes. And Mrs Thatcher, of course, was talking up global warming in the late eighties, when nobody else – certainly not Blair or – and isn't everyone pro-science now, bar the odd Catholic lunatic. Sorry, you're not – not Catholic? So no, today's not about politics, it's about climate.

TESSA. Whatever prevails today will be everything to do with politics and nothing to do with the weather.

Pause.

JENKS. Right. Actually, climate's not synonymous with… No. Evidently you're more in the know than I.

TESSA. I know David's in two minds and wishes to look single-minded. I know that. I know none of us want to appear to be on the wrong side of you. More punch?

She pours him some.

JENKS. Are you buttering me up?

TESSA. How could I? You say you're entirely independent.

JENKS. Of course.

TESSA. You argued passionately for the Climate-Change Bill, pushing for eighty not sixty per cent CO_2 reductions –

JENKS. Carbon equivalent –

TESSA. Sorry?

JENKS. Nothing.

TESSA. You raised the alarm about impacts on biodiversity, argued for a mixed-energy economy including nuclear, fell out with Miliband Two a bit about Europe's role and you've now published a book online: *Keeping Cool: The Facts of Anthropogenic Climate Change.* Quite a mouthful.

JENKS. I get incredibly angry about this glib use of words. We are addressing the anthropogenic dimension of climate change, because we have as much chance of addressing climate change in itself as voting for a white Christmas.

Sorry, I do, as I say, get angry about that.

TESSA. The thing is, Colin, there are bound to be questions hanging over you. At this time.

JENKS. With a new Government, of course, everything must be questioned –

TESSA. But after last night –

JENKS. No, sorry, we need to be very clear about this: last night was a localised event.

TESSA. Local, of course, but with wider implications.

JENKS. No, very clear: the events in Bristol should have no further bearing on policy.

Pause.

TESSA. Chris tends to like his own people, just as David does.

I mean, for some of us in the party it's quite hard to take. I know it's a cliché to say they went to school together but they went to school together; they went to Oxford together, the PM went to Brasenose, Chris, Balliol; the PM studied PPE, Chris, History; the PM went into communications, Chris investment banking; the PM has a family home in Oxfordshire, Chris has a family home in Norfolk; the PM has a Lexus, Chris has a Prius... Do you see a pattern, Colin?

Maybe you and I need to form our own axis.

Pause.

JENKS. Well, I suppose the problem with that might be that we don't actually know whether we agree with each other. About anything.

TESSA. True, very true.

What do you hope for – from today?

JENKS. Today?

TESSA. In policy terms?

JENKS. As little change as possible.

  I think we probably have the policy about right actually.

TESSA. Would I agree were I paddling through my living room in Bristol?

JENKS. We need to remain steadfast.

TESSA. But we're a young Government, Colin, with a crisis on our watch. David'll want new narratives, not 'If it ain't broke don't fix it.'

JENKS. Well, if you're after novelty for its own sake –

TESSA. Chris'll naturally want to retain ownership of his ministry. I don't intend simply to play bad cop to his good. Not that I give a stuff about popularity. But resilience is pretty procedural stuff.

JENKS. That's arguable.

TESSA. What is?

JENKS. I mean, it depends on one's definition of the term… resilience.

TESSA. Go on.

JENKS. I myself think the message we need to keep rolling out with dogged consistency is about changing habits, mitigation – but, you could, you know, take a dimmer view of all that.

TESSA. Could you be a little less gnomic?

JENKS. I just mean you could suggest that from now on climate-change policy is less about heading off the coming storm and more about weathering its worst effects.

TESSA. Is that your view?

JENKS. I think it a little gloomy myself. But were I, say, in Bangladesh…

TESSA. Or Bristol?

  Her BlackBerry pings.

Ah. Okay. It's the boss. Pre-meet.

I'm hardly his cup of tea. Too frumpy.

But oddly enough I might be more what this country needs right now than the Eton boys. Like you, I'm bloody good on detail.

She shuts down her laptop which she then squirrels away.

Yes, there he is again, I need to go. Rather like being electronically tagged.

I should know, I introduced the things.

Finish the punch, I'm replete.

She leaves. JENKS *pours out the drink.*

JENKS. Thanks. Tessa.

A moment. SARIKA *enters.*

SARIKA. Oh. Colin. Should you be here?

JENKS. Of course. Punctual as ever.

SARIKA. No, you're fine.

JENKS. Braced for the coming purge? Oh yes, they'll be casting around for scapegoats today.

He kisses her.

Just had that reactionary dominatrix working me over.

SARIKA. Tessa? What was she doing here?

JENKS. Don't let on I voted Liberal Democrat.

What a shower! I said Casson had nothing in his track record to suggest any interest, concern, flair even for this issue and his performance last night only confirms it –

SARIKA. Colin, can I be very rude and ask if I can have this room for a moment?

JENKS. You naturally dislike Tories but you kind of think in Government they might be indistinguishable from –

SARIKA. Colin, I have to ready this room –

She's clearing up his drying cycling gear.

JENKS. Right. Sure. I could go to my – actually do I have my new office?

I could perch in the old one.

SARIKA. Use mine.

JENKS. Well, okay, I'll repair to your office then.

Same as before?

SARIKA. No. In there.

JENKS. Through there? But that's my – I mean, I still have the key for that.

SARIKA. Maybe I should have that –

JENKS. What?

SARIKA. Your key.

JENKS. My key? Of course.

Slightly dazed he starts working the key off his keyring.

I am feeling slightly pushed about, Sarika.

SARIKA. I know. It's insane right now.

JENKS. I mean, you ask me in, in the middle of the night –

SARIKA. Did I ask you in?

Pause.

JENKS. Oh, shitty shit – I can't – get – this.

He throws his keyring down.

SARIKA. Keep it. No hurry. Pop it in internal post.

JENKS. Look, you and I are the institutional memory of this place, don't forget that. I mean, these guys are chancers. In by a snicket. Patchy mandate. Bringing in people from totally inappropriate backgrounds – line of command is a mess –

SARIKA. Colin, I need this room like five minutes ago, okay?

I'm sorry if that sounds rude.

He looks at her; then seizes his stuff, bar his helmet.

JENKS. You seem to have forgotten certain crucial facts, namely that I am the most respected climatologist in the UK, ranked third globally, that I chair, have chaired three panels of the IPCC, that I am Master of Trinity College, and that you, you are a senior Civil Servant.

SARIKA. Okay. Thanks for putting me straight on that, Colin.

He exits through the inner door; she waits, then goes out, returning shortly afterwards with WILL, *looking slightly befuddled, who carries some documents.*

This is it.

WILL. Wow.

It's hardly the Oval Office.

Was that him?

SARIKA. Oh yes.

WILL. Fuck! Part of me wants to kick his head in. Now.

SARIKA. Will, you don't bring any baggage to this, do you understand?

WILL. Yes. Sure.

SARIKA. Behind all the bumbling and bluff there is steel. You read the briefings?

WILL. Hard to care about all these personalities and offices and who answers to who.

SARIKA. Well, love, you'd better start caring 'cos that's the territory now.

He nods, looks expectantly at her.

Look, you're half-asleep, I know I am.

WILL. I should have shaved, right?

SARIKA. No, it's fine. Makes you look more authentic. Grizzled.

You look really… good.

WILL. Really?

She moves closer to him. They almost kiss.

SARIKA. That would be – a mistake.

WILL. Your call, of course.

SARIKA. If we were to be –

WILL. You look amazing. You are amazing.

SARIKA. Will.

WILL. Seventy-two hours ago I was in a bunk bed, in an ice storm, utterly alone and then last night I'm in your bed, okay, alone again, thinking how did I end up in this amazing woman's bed? Albeit alone.

SARIKA. I'm sorry, love, there's barely been a minute –

WILL. We shouldn't have gone home yesterday.

SARIKA. Look, try to forget about yesterday.

WILL. Right, forget I hit my fucking dad?

Forget my own mother lying to me for practically my entire life? Okay.

SARIKA. Everything was confused, the drink, the storm, they didn't mean what they said.

WILL. Fuck!

SARIKA. What?

WILL. I need to check if the storm hit them.

SARIKA. It's okay. I did. No extensive damage in Norfolk.

WILL. Right. Good. Good.

Dad'll be disappointed.

They laugh.

SARIKA. He's such a scary guy.

WILL. Never realised how scary 'til now.

SARIKA. Scarily like you.

WILL. Like me? Thanks.

SARIKA. His passion. His pathological conviction.

WILL. Do you think he's mad?

SARIKA. No. Obsessive maybe –

WILL. Last night I thought he'd lost it.

   Truly. And I saw myself in it too.

   Don't let me become like that.

SARIKA. There's no danger of that, none.

   Look, when this is done we should go back, try again –

WILL. No, no way –

SARIKA. For your mum at least –

   I'll set it up. She was okay to me.

   I'll call her, I'm not proud.

WILL. No, she'll not go against him. It's a one-party state there. Dad's word is law.

   I'm the quisling, I'm Judas now.

SARIKA. Will, if bringing you in here cuts you off from them I won't forgive myself. Your father's right, maybe this is a mistake –

WILL. Mistake! Love, this is no mistake, this, this is the best thing I have ever done.

   She suddenly kisses him; it gets passionate; she pulls away.

SARIKA. Will, you know this is not what this is about.

WILL. Oh, I completely recognise that.

SARIKA. We have to get to business. Is my lipstick – shit, I – look, you read my paper at least?

WILL. Yep. It's good. It's very… stylish.

SARIKA. You saw I imported pictures of you in it, from my visit to the Antarctic, on the Larsen B –

WILL. Did you tell me you'd make public use – ?

SARIKA. I mean, it's just internal now –

WILL. Right.

SARIKA. It's mainly the gospel according to Jenks, but I figure we use it as a stalking horse – and it's crucial we don't play anything as a 'fait accomplit' with Chris, not that it is –

WILL. Right – sorry, Sarika, hang on –

SARIKA. What?

WILL. I'm sorry, just, that, that's wrong, this –

SARIKA. What?

WILL. 'An Expedition onto the West Antarctic Ice Sheet.'

SARIKA. Yes, that's where you took me…

WILL. That's where I took you, yes, but this, this is the Brunt Ice Sheet.

SARIKA. But, Will, no one'll – I mean, it's just – a, you know, totally white –

WILL. Anyone serious will know by the inclination, the environs –

SARIKA. Oh, be serious –

WILL. I'm being highly serious –

SARIKA. We don't need professional vanity now –

WILL. I think I should know as I am –

SARIKA. – and it's only a draft –

WILL. – I just mean if it's untrue, even this –

SARIKA. – and we don't need all this referred guilt. From your father.

WILL. I'm sorry?

SARIKA. Okay. There, look, I can change it, hang on: 'The...
Brunt... Ice Sheet.'

There. Copy it about. Done.

WILL. Just, you said something about – Dad.

SARIKA. Your dad only tried to do what you're doing.

WILL. He betrayed the data.

Betrayed his vocation.

SARIKA. He came in here, like you. To tell the truth to power.
Too soon, yes, too raw, untimely, yes. But he had the balls to
cross that line. And now it's you. Today, today is your
chance to make good for everything he failed to do.

WILL. Yeah. Right. To... atone. Yes.

Pause.

SARIKA. So we have to sort some preliminaries – have a
shufty on this – here –

She spreads some papers on the table. WILL *looks at them
sleepily.*

WILL. God, I'm all over the shop.

SARIKA. Well, do you trust me to sign them unseen?

WILL. Of course, I –

SARIKA. I mean, they could roast me for bringing you in, I've
ridden roughshod over procedure, so I'd quite understand –

WILL. Sarika, what you said, you know, when you came to me,
clarified things for me, clarified. It's easy when you're down
there, in all that... ice... that nothingness... so far from...
this, from people, to think, to imagine what you're doing is
simply science, but it's not, it's more than that, you're, like
you said, you're answerable to the world, what you know
must be shared, must be accounted for – is this making sense?

She touches him lightly.

SARIKA. So, look, you'll need to sign a couple of things, here, and here, just with reference to this meeting, largely about the intellectual property of what transpires – in here –

WILL. But my research is my –

SARIKA. No, no, it's not about your research.

WILL. I have to be clear about that, Sar.

SARIKA. Will, don't call me that here, okay?

WILL. Okay.

SARIKA. Look, you don't have any record of – you know you've not mouthed off for, say, Friends of the Earth –

WILL. Oh, I can't stick Friends of the Earth – so manipulative –

SARIKA. 'Cos that's one of the disclaimers, here –

WILL. What?

SARIKA. Just that you wouldn't go and use anything that emerges to any NGO or political group –

WILL. I thought this was just an initial –

SARIKA. Will, you know about Triple C?

WILL. Triple what?

SARIKA. Sorry – Civil Contingency Committee?

WILL. Yeah. Err. No. Don't they meet to do – what – terrorism – stuff like terrorism?

SARIKA. Triple C deal with crises. Today is a crisis. Okay, the waters have retreated in Bristol but we know this will happen again and again.

This room is one of a suite of rooms dedicated to crisis management.

The phones are part of a network of lines immune to any collapse of communications; these lines are connected to the entire country: emergency workers, Met Office Environment Agency – should the sort of scenarios you've predicted befall us, we gather here, the doors sealed, and we become in

effect in a cockpit preserved to administer and secure the
health and safety of the British Isles.

WILL. Right. Right. Wow.

I am feeling a little out of my depth here.

SARIKA. We all are, Will, we all are, and that's the absolute
point.

So you'll say what we agreed, say it categorically, with
certainty?

WILL. Of course, I'll have to stress that nothing is entirely
certain, of course, and that events will play out in confusing,
often counterintuitive ways –

SARIKA. Will, can I make an observation – from now on,
there's no time for qualifications. For ambiguities. Which I
know, I know exist.

From now on, everything must be said clearly and firmly.

WILL. Of course.

SARIKA. And another thing – you don't mention what we
know – about the past.

WILL. How do you mean?

SARIKA. Any animus between you and Colin will weaken your
case.

WILL. He suppressed the data!

SARIKA. For the purposes of today, you and I barely know
each other and what happened between Colin and your father
is irrelevant. Promise me. Promise me.

WILL *nods*.

WILL. Weird. Always think of myself as a hard, essentially cold
person. But look at me, I'm a mooning bundle of nerves.

SARIKA. Will, this could be one of the most important
meetings in the history of this country, comparable to
Churchill in 1940, say, Blair after 9/11 –

Her phone alarm goes.

So, look, you need to sign. Here.

And here.

And here also.

He does.

Now go for a walk in St James's Park –

WILL. It's raining.

SARIKA. Okay, there's a canteen, in the basement, go there, have a think, have a coffee, a read. Come back in an hour. Go, Will. And thank you.

WILL *makes as if to kiss her, she shakes her head, he turns and, as he exits, he walks into* CHRIS *entering with an armful of books, clutching a coffee; the books get scattered about.*

CHRIS. Careful! Jesus.

WILL. Sorry.

CHRIS. Sorry?

SARIKA. Yes, be careful.

WILL. As I say –

CHRIS. Look, my suit –

SARIKA. I can get that off –

WILL. Sorry.

CHRIS. – coffee on – George fucking – Monbiot.

Shit. Skinny latte too. Doubt he'd approve.

WILL. I'm really very sorry.

SARIKA. Stop saying sorry.

WILL. Can I get you a replacement – coffee?

CHRIS. Forget it. Tasted like oxtail soup. With milk.

WILL *lingers;* SARIKA *nods for him to go.* CHRIS *is taking off his trousers.*

SARIKA. Chris, let me take those –

CHRIS. You object to the jockey pants?

SARIKA. I just have some wet wipes.

CHRIS. She objects to the jockey pants.

Birthday present from Mum.

Wonderfully permeable. I do think it's important to minimise sweat in the groin region – I hope, Sarika, this won't come back as sexual harassment.

SARIKA. Here.

She takes his trousers. He stands, unabashed in his jockey pants, then picks up the scattered books.

I'll get a storage heater –

CHRIS. You saw me holding forth on News 24?

SARIKA (*off*). You were impressive.

CHRIS. Cunts put me in kneehigh wellies and dragged me round this housing estate in Avonmouth; I must have looked a right arse in a high-vis jacket and galoshes mumbling some crap about a 'wake-up call'. Did I look an arse?

SARIKA (*off*). Got you on the front pages of the late editions. Did you read the books?

CHRIS. Mmm. Skim read.

Knew Monbiot at Oxford actually; shagged anything from a state school – and this one, *Six Degrees* – is there a prize for writing the most dismal book ever published, a Booker for sheer lugubriousness – gave up after three degrees; Lovelock, okay – he is certifiably crazy which in the end has its amusing side, got quite giggly at the thought of a white paper proposing shifting freight to solar yachts, compulsory vat-grown soya for all and relocating the populace to Greenland – cheers, Jim!

SARIKA. And my paper?

CHRIS. Oh, and then your briefing paper. Which was at least – brief.

She's re-entered with a heater.

SARIKA. Just an attempt to summarise…

CHRIS. Sure.

SARIKA. Nothing in there's set in stone.

She drapes the trousers over a chair.

CHRIS. You're probably thinking he should have done all this before accepting the post, right?

SARIKA. Not at all.

CHRIS. Well, I said I didn't want to rush in. I don't do that. I talk to the team. I take soundings. Right?

SARIKA. I think that makes a lot of sense.

CHRIS. Yeah, well, I hope you do.

And what exactly is a PIGG?

SARIKA. Sorry? Oh, as in P-I-G-G?

CHRIS. As in P-I-G-G.

SARIKA. Potent Industrial Greenhouse Gas.

CHRIS. 'Potent Industrial Greenhouse Gas.'

SARIKA. Such as CFCs, HCFCs, HFCs –

CHRIS. Wait, wait –

SARIKA. Sulphur hexagonide, nitrous oxide –

CHRIS. Memo: you're talking to the guy whose last chemistry report concluded: 'Too lethargic to inspire confidence.' PIGGs!

SARIKA. We can stick to GHGs.

CHRIS. Greenhouse gases? You see, I am not content like some to keep it global.

I'm a detail man.

SARIKA. Absolutely.

CHRIS. Is there a strain of Tourette's where you spout acronyms rather than obscenities? 'The EUETS is implemented by the ERU who distribute EUAs.' Translation, please.

SARIKA. The European Union Emission Trading Scheme is implemented by the Emission Reduction Unit who distribute European Union Allowances.

CHRIS. Do you ever read this stuff aloud?

SARIKA. It's not intended for public recitation.

CHRIS *looks at her.*

CHRIS. Okay, good answer, well done.

Yeah, learned a lot from this when the acronyms abated. Page ten, learned that the atmosphere was a fluid, which was a bit of a shock.

SARIKA. Of course. Vapour, gas –

CHRIS. Page twelve, learned there's an enormous stock of methane about to fart out of Siberia, area as big as Western Europe about to let rip one enormous fart; page fourteen, I learn to my dismay the tropical zone just got a whole lot bigger which sounded okay, but no, no, more cyclones, more killer waves and failing rains; and then on page fifteen, we learn the sea's gone a bit funny too, oh yes, there's these indolent yet essential little plankton in it who've quit their Gaian task of sopping up all that CO2 and are now emitting it; and then to cap it all, page seventeen, we learn the fucking rainforest, despite Sting's best efforts, is dying on its feet and oh, by the way, that's another carbon sink gone and and and – am I alone in finding all this profoundly dispiriting? It's like going to your GP with a sniff and getting diagnosed with Avian Flu.

SARIKA. You're concentrating on the diagnostic section. The hope's in the prognostic.

CHRIS. Oh, sure, after the Four Horseman of the Apocalypse make merry, in hobbles the European Union Emission Trading Scheme. I mean, where are the solutions?

Nothing in here could have seen off last night. Where, as every fucker is asking me, is the contingency plan?

Pause.

SARIKA. Well, if it's no good it's all we've got.

If we stay mainstream.

CHRIS. Am I right in thinking that our task, our duty is to make this planet a place to live on rather than just survive on?

SARIKA. I think that's right.

CHRIS. Then this isn't up to snuff, is it?

Pause.

SARIKA. So what do you want – if you don't want this?

CHRIS. Top question, Sarika.

But then you've been on this one five years, right, whereas I started, what, ten days ago?

SARIKA. Yeah.

CHRIS. I mean, am I not entitled to ask what you actually achieved in this ministry?

'Cos Bristol's gonna shine a great fuck-off light in here and I need to know what to defend and what to disown.

Give me the audit. What did you lot achieve?

SARIKA. An enormous amount actually.

CHRIS. Yes, but on paper or in actuality?

SARIKA. Absolutely in actuality, in actions.

CHRIS. Actual actions?

SARIKA. Actual actions, yes.

CHRIS. Okay, so how much power comes from renewables? I mean, we're meant to be, what, according to policy, getting to ten per cent, right? Fifteen by, when, 2020. So where are we at right now on that?

SARIKA. Huge growth year on year.

CHRIS. Yeah, but what is the actual percentage achieved right now?

SARIKA. Right now it's very hard to precisely determine –

CHRIS. Sarika; this isn't *Newsnight*, okay. What percentage? Ten?

SARIKA. No, not ten, not yet.

CHRIS. Five, then?

SARIKA. Depending on whether you –

CHRIS. Five per cent?

SARIKA. If you include offsetting we might be able to talk about in the vicinity of, at best, let's say… four per cent.

CHRIS. Four per cent?

SARIKA. That's optimistic, that's taking in, that's –

CHRIS. Not even four per cent!

SARIKA. The planning system has been against us.

And investment's crashed in the recession –

CHRIS. Okay, scratch renewables then. Is there any discernible reduction in, say, road use?

SARIKA. Well, some indicators suggest –

CHRIS. I asked a very simple question.

SARIKA. Road use.

CHRIS. Yes?

SARIKA. Road use is on the increase.

CHRIS. Electric cars, say?

SARIKA. Research into electric cars is going slowly too.

CHRIS. What about, those, thingy, those –

SARIKA. Biofuels?

CHRIS. Apparently a bit shit, right?

SARIKA. In practice they create another tier of problem.

CHRIS. And – aviation – don't tell me, new runways, increased passenger flights?

SARIKA. Yes. Yes.

CHRIS. How about reducing household carbon emissions?

SARIKA. That's more local authorities, Chris.

CHRIS. Under our direction, right?

SARIKA. Yes, but also international protocols –

CHRIS. But you say here we need to start the exit from fossil fuels from, what, 2015! Whilst idly mentioning the oil's run out, the water's run dry and we're breeding ourselves to extinction.

SARIKA. None of which is actually our brief.

CHRIS. 2015! That's less than five years and you've been on it for five years and you got to four per cent renewables and a couple of market towns free from the scourge of plastic bags!

Pause.

SARIKA. From one point of – actually, yes it is, yes I do think it's – crap. Actually.

CHRIS. I don't see you saying that in here. Sorry.

SARIKA. Well, we respond to you, we don't invent in a vacuum. So what do you want, Minister?

Because this, here, this is the consensus, this is the conventional wisdom, so if you don't want this, you better know what you do want.

CHRIS. Right. Okay. Well, I'll be totally honest with you, Sarika, right now I actually don't know.

SARIKA. Right.

He puts on the trousers which have dried.

CHRIS. I mean, when Dave called and offered the ministry I went deaf, all the sound went. I knew he was still speaking

but I couldn't make out the drift of his words, it was just sound.

I still said yes, of course.

Wish I'd listened harder. To the brief.

Now he lands fucking Tessa Fortnum on me. Claims it's a strengthening, I know it's a warning.

SARIKA. Who do I answer to? I don't seem to have an opposite number.

CHRIS. Yeah, Tessa tends to bypass the Civil Service until forced to acknowledge them. Hates my guts but never mind.

It should have been made clear she was to be junior minister but Dave fudged it. Scares the crap out of him too. You know her majority hasn't wavered in twenty years, not at all, through Major, New Labour, everything.

He claims she's there so we don't frighten people off, post-Bristol. Claims she has the undying love of Worcester Woman and her coven – sorry, is that misogynist?

SARIKA. A bit. Her track record's pretty right-wing.

CHRIS. Ooh, just a trifle! All schools should be faith schools – Rowan Williams blushed at that; reinstate conscription to end knife crime. Don't get her started on immigration.

But the thing is, she worries me less than Jenks. He's behind this, isn't he?

SARIKA. Colin's driven the analysis. As you'd expect.

CHRIS. Mmm. I do hate a beardy expert. And how good is he, exactly?

SARIKA. Colin?

CHRIS. Because we might well need to throw someone to the pack.

How do we know he's fit for purpose?

SARIKA. He's generally acknowledged to be the top in his field.

CHRIS. According to whom?

SARIKA. Well, to – to his peers.

CHRIS. According to his chums. How do we know we can trust him?

Nobody voted for him.

SARIKA. Nobody voted for me either.

CHRIS. At least I can sack you –

SARIKA. Well. You can sack Colin.

CHRIS. He takes a salary? Good.

SARIKA. There's never been any question from Government or scientific circles that he was anything but the natural choice.

CHRIS. That's what bothers me about this. It's all so fucking chummy – we've got a major climate-driven catastrophe on our watch and the country needs to know it's not in the hands of a bunch of procrastinating wankers.

I need *my* scientist. Someone fresh, someone who speaks my language, someone ahead of the curve.

SARIKA. Right.

Pause.

I might have someone. Pretty left-field.

CHRIS. No new agers. And no one beaky like Dawkins.

SARIKA. I know one of the few in the field who actively disagrees with Colin.

CHRIS. Personal reasons or scientific ones?

SARIKA. Chiefly scientific.

CHRIS. Okay. Is he young?

SARIKA. Yes.

CHRIS. Is he political?

SARIKA. Total political virgin.

CHRIS. I'm liking it. Telegenic?

SARIKA. Could be.

CHRIS. Loyal?

SARIKA. Incorruptible. Apparently.

CHRIS. You know him?

SARIKA. Yes, I know him.

CHRIS. Did he just spill coffee on George Monbiot and me?

Pause.

SARIKA. I invited him in, Minister.

CHRIS. Without asking me first?

SARIKA. Yes.

CHRIS. Without informing Tessa?

SARIKA. Yes.

CHRIS. Or Jenks?

SARIKA. Yes.

Pause.

CHRIS. It was suggested I move you.

SARIKA. Of course.

CHRIS. It was also suggested that you were indispensable.

But you know what, nobody's indispensable.

SARIKA. If you want me to go I will get you a wonderful replacement.

Silence; CHRIS looks at SARIKA.

CHRIS. Sarika, do you love this country?

SARIKA. I'm sorry?

CHRIS. I mean the land, the land itself.

SARIKA. Oh. Really?

CHRIS. Yes.

SARIKA. Oh dear. Do I love the land?

CHRIS. Where did you grow up?

She looks genuinely surprised.

SARIKA. Sorry, how is this relevant, Chris?

CHRIS. Oh, I think it's highly relevant.

SARIKA. Okay. I grew up in Rugby.

CHRIS. Does Rugby inspire any particular sentiments in you?

SARIKA. Sentiments? Well. Dismay.

Do you think I'm disloyal or something?

CHRIS. My love for this country comes out in the strangest
ways, you know, such as my affection for the avocet – do
you know the avocet, little curved bill, black and white, real
quirky little character; I consider the avocet the
quintessential English bird, I think 'avocet' and immediately
I see, what, a levee over a salt marsh, a network of creeks,
the distant North Sea as dark as flint, a walk against a wind
on a darkening day, entering a smoke-riddled pub and
drinking a pint of Norfolk ale.

The reason I am here, the reason I am endangering my
already imperilled marriage and why I have taken a two-
hundred per cent cut in income is to defend that avocet and
all it brings in its train from change – climate change – but
any change truly because frankly I can imagine no alteration
of any of that which is not a diminishment.

What's his name?

SARIKA. Who?

CHRIS. Your scientist…

SARIKA. I'm not his – he's not my scientist.

CHRIS. What's his name?

SARIKA. Dr Paxton.

CHRIS. And you met him, where?

SARIKA. A field trip. To Antarctica.

CHRIS. What fun! Did you have intimate relations in his sleeping bag?

SARIKA. I object to that.

CHRIS. Just a little quip. You wouldn't do anything so stupid.

Pause.

SARIKA. Will predicted a Bristol event, he said, something of this scale would happen in the next thousand days –

CHRIS. Nostradamus – and sexy too.

SARIKA. And because it's so clear, so precise, it's very inspiring, what he has to say.

CHRIS. I obviously need to meet him, sample his appeal.

Pause.

Bring him in. To this meeting.

SARIKA. Right. I understand.

CHRIS. You chair it.

SARIKA. That's not procedure…

CHRIS. Smuggling hunky boffins into Whitehall's not procedure but these are interesting times.

Yes, you chair. Let Tessa think I'm giving her room.

And I need a replacement coffee and fresh trousers and then, then – we go.

CHRIS *starts to go.*

But if he turns out to be the problem rather than the solution, there will be consequences.

SARIKA. Naturally.

CHRIS. Okay. Oh, by the way. It's my birthday today.

How about a cake and some candles?

SARIKA. How many? I mean, how many candles?

CHRIS. I'll leave that to your discretion.

He goes off.

Scene Two

Later, the same.

SARIKA, CHRIS, TESSA *are seated, eating cake; a birthday cake in the middle of the table, candles lit.* JENKS *is standing.*

JENKS. What is resilience?

The ecological definition is clear: 'The capacity of a system to maintain its stability in the face of change and external shocks.'

Resilience is, in effect, stability.

Suddenly he sets off a rape alarm.

CHRIS. What the bloody hell are you – doing?

SARIKA. Colin, that'll alert – security.

CHRIS. Switch the thing off.

JENKS *stops the alarm;* TESSA *chuckles.*

JENKS. False alarm, of course. But isn't your response indicative? Heart rates are up, pulse racing, adrenalin up. You turn on the cause of panic itself and you become the problem. So it is in our reactions to extreme climate events such as Bristol. We register shock: 'This can't be happening!' Then anger: 'Why wasn't I told?' Then false diagnoses: 'Something could have been done.' Misinformed actions ensue and so we reach the final stage, Learned Passivity: 'Nothing can be done.' Resilience is thereby utterly depleted.

Can I ask you all to stand?

Just for a moment, please?

An awkward pause; CHRIS stands; then SARIKA. TESSA stands, smiles.

Isn't it interesting how even the smallest change generates resistance?

I'd like you to close your eyes. That's it.

All of you. Good. Good.

Okay. Imagine you're a native English wood, that you're the flora and fauna of this wood, which survives on its own terms and is entirely, as it were, resilient.

Now you can be any one of the following elements of that system: soil, tree, mammal, insect.

A ripple of laughter.

Chris, what do you fancy?

CHRIS. Me?

JENKS. Yes.

CHRIS. Oh. What do you recommend, Colin?

JENKS. How about a tree? Top of the species ladder. Highly evolved.

CHRIS. Very flattering.

Can I be an oak?

JENKS. An oak it is.

He places a Post-it note on CHRIS.

Sarika?

SARIKA. Am I allowed in an ancient English wood?

JENKS. Don't be daft.

SARIKA. Okay, I'll be a bird then.

JENKS. A thrush?

CHRIS *laughs.*

SARIKA. Colin, is that your idea of a joke?

JENKS. A mistle thrush then.

And, Tessa, perhaps you'll be kind enough to be soil, itself a form of life.

TESSA. We're all clay in the end.

JENKS. There – all the elements of a resilient system.

WILL enters looking flustered.

WILL. Sorry.

JENKS. This is a private meeting.

SARIKA. No, it's okay, this is –

TESSA. Yes, private, surely.

CHRIS. It's fine. Come in.

TESSA. Are we expecting someone?

SARIKA. I –

CHRIS. Yes. We're expecting someone.

TESSA. Oh. I see.

She looks at JENKS.

Would it not be a courtesy to Colin at least to know who this is?

JENKS. I know who it is. William.

SARIKA. Dr William Paxton.

WILL. Will, please.

SARIKA. From BAS.

CHRIS. Acronym.

SARIKA. British Antarctic Survey.

WILL. I'm a glaciologist.

JENKS. Rob's lad.

CHRIS. You know each other?

SARIKA. This is Professor Colin Jenks.

WILL. Yes. I know.

JENKS. Last time I saw you, you were, what, postgrad?

WILL *nods*.

Will's dad is a very old pal of mine.

CHRIS. I expect he's wondering who I am –

SARIKA. So, sorry, so – this is Christopher Casson, Minister for Climate Change and – well, and –

TESSA. And?

SARIKA. And this is – sorry, Tessa –

TESSA. Tessa Fortnum.

SARIKA *and* TESSA. Minister for Resilience.

WILL. Right. Hullo.

TESSA. Hello.

WILL. Again, apologies for interrupting –

He drops his things. CHRIS *frowns at* SARIKA.

TESSA. We were just being creatures of the native English wood.

JENKS. We could actually do with another ecological link, Will, do you fancy being some kind of micro-organism?

WILL. I don't generally do this sort of thing.

CHRIS. Hardly my forte either.

JENKS. An earthworm perhaps?

WILL. A worm?

Fine.

JENKS. Good – and now we form the web of resilience! I have here the proverbial piece of string, which I'll give you, Tessa, given you're the primary force of life, and then to you, Will, as a driver of soil decomposition, and then of course to Chris,

the tree, supporter of the living soil (and also a carbon sink, as is the soil, never forget that), and then over here to Sarika browsing on the tree. Hold it tight if you would; there; and here; and there; hold it tightly; here and here; connecting you – to you – to you – and again – tree to soil; soil to worm; worm to thrush; thrush to soil again; now, there –

He has created a great cat's cradle of string.

Now pull tighter. See how tough the web of life is.

CHRIS. Impedes your blood flow certainly.

JENKS. This is resilience. Mutual aid. And so it is in human society too; imagine a small town – the mutual interests, the relations – but now, look, look, here comes change, climate change or otherwise and look –

He cuts a string.

– your oak dies; two degrees of warming, and the oak dies; the web is weaker but it holds; but unprotected, the soil's too hot, it dries out, and now all flora shrivels and so the worm starves and so the thrush goes hungry too, flies further, breeds less, and little by little the wood dies.

CHRIS. How is this relevant exactly, Colin?

JENKS. See it as an analogy for events such as Bristol. Because Bristol has revealed the total absence of resilience in modern Britain.

TESSA. Absence of moral fibre, perhaps?

JENKS. Well, I don't tend to use moral terms.

CHRIS. Bristol's a natural disaster.

WILL. With anthropogenic causes.

JENKS. Hard to say, isn't it, Will. After only twelve hours.

WILL. And events such as Bristol will from now on be the norm rather than the exception.

They all look at him.

JENKS. No, I don't think anyone is really saying that.

CHRIS. Well, he just did.

Pause.

SARIKA. Shall we look a little closer, then? At what data we have? If, Colin, you've –

JENKS. That was just the opening of – a sort of warm-up.

SARIKA. But as we are pushed for time?

TESSA. What were you going to say, Colin?

CHRIS. He can chip in as we go.

JENKS. I was hoping to give a sustained account of the behavioural basis of the whole response to anthropogenic –

CHRIS. Anthropowhat?

SARIKA. Man-made climate change – Colin has this bugbear about –

JENKS. I do not 'have this' – the entire scientific community take great care in how they –

TESSA. So you were going on to say –

SARIKA. You were going to say Bristol was a one in one-hundred-year event to be expected and the only thing to consider is the level of preparedness and the fact you consider it a diversion from the slow ongoing task of reducing emissions house by house, person by person, through treaties and law and science-based policies?

Sorry – to paraphrase.

JENKS. You put it rather well.

Okay, maybe I should just, as you say, 'chip in' then.

He packs his things away.

SARIKA. Thanks, thanks, Colin.

Okay, as we know, the flood zone was largely in communities west of the city.

JENKS. Already deemed to be on land rated Flood Risk Three.

TESSA. Meaning?

JENKS. Meaning sub-prime floodplain land.

CHRIS. Largely social housing as far as I could see.

TESSA. Notorious for crime, antisocial behaviour.

JENKS. I mean, these areas get flooded, sea-level rise or no.
Dodgy developers.

SARIKA. But tides were obviously a factor here.

JENKS. Obviously a factor.

SARIKA *shows them a series of print-outs of images.*

SARIKA. These are satellite images of the tidal bore coming in;
that's 21.50, it's fairly minor, building up around Lynmouth;
now 22.10 at Clevedon, it's doubled in height; now as it hits the
Avon and the estuary narrows it reaches the maximum height.

CHRIS. That's a bloody tsunami, isn't it?

JENKS. What's barely been explained is it's a naturally
occurring tidal surge that appears on a monthly basis.

CHRIS. But how high's that bugger there?

SARIKA. At that point they say four metres –

WILL. A metre over the highest recorded previous bore.

JENKS. As high as a metre? I doubt that.

WILL. The impact confirms it.

TESSA. Youngsters surf on it.

SARIKA. It's been unusually swollen all year but according to
the Environment Agency this has no precedent.

JENKS. It could be explained by a lot of dredging in the Bristol
Channel; sea-level rise is unlikely to be the driver of this –

WILL. Sea-level rise is the decisive factor.

JENKS. How can you say that? The Severn's affected by mid-
Atlantic currents and westerlies, I mean, this is hardly going
to be about polar melt.

TESSA. I took Colin's point to be less about causes and more about our capacity to react.

JENKS. Indeed. Ripeness is all.

CHRIS. The reaction was clearly bloody atrocious.

TESSA. I witnessed youths attacking the emergency services.

Appalling traffic management. Bottlenecked roads. Breathtaking unreadiness. Helicopters couldn't achieve landfall.

CHRIS. It's an indictment of the fucking local authority.

TESSA. Labour, naturally.

SARIKA. No overall control. I think.

TESSA. Even the storm drains were blocked.

CHRIS. You saw a great deal more than me, clearly.

JENKS. So, okay, we need to build resilience from the bottom up.

TESSA. Which might then be about the balance.

The balance between us, Chris.

CHRIS *looks at* TESSA.

CHRIS. Dr Paxton's keeping his counsel.

WILL. Well. Everything I say has to be taken in the context of the fact I have been on field study in the Antarctic until seventy-two hours ago and for personal reasons last night I was in Norfolk –

CHRIS. Me too. Until the flood. Where abouts?

WILL. Oh. Hunstanton way. My parents are –

CHRIS. We're nearer Sheringham.

WILL. Well, anyway, as a consequence I can't comment on absolute specifics.

TESSA. Sorry, isn't that actually what we're here to discuss?

SARIKA. But you've been observing the ice. In Antartica.

WILL. My team and I, yes, have been working on building a model for – hang on, maybe it's easier if I –

He starts unzipping his laptop, spreading a miscellany of documents on the desk.

JENKS. Okay, so you're here to offer an update – on melt-rates?

WILL. Well, Sarika asked me –

TESSA. You know Ms Chatterjee?

SARIKA. Evidently.

TESSA. You didn't just stumble in here with your laptop?

CHRIS. It's okay, Tessa, Sarika, I think I'm right in saying, visited Will –

TESSA. Oh, I see, you're rather more in the loop.

CHRIS. The team, our team need to be proactive.

TESSA. But there seems to be rather a lot of backstory.

JENKS. I can at any time source you that data, but I'm sure Will has his own people, his own methodology. Generally we customise it exactly to Government need.

WILL. I have to a degree simplified.

JENKS. Well, Will, we don't simplify, we simply filter out what's not fit for purpose. We figure ministers are busy people –

SARIKA. Will, you could just talk to us –

WILL. Okay, it's just – sure, okay I was going to talk through the basics of climate through the Holocene, the last ten-thousand-odd years and rehearse some of the properties and dynamics of ice behaviour, bearing in mind some of this will skimp specifics, oh, and meteorological models factoring in some variables stemming from our models of flow and melt patterns, focusing on our work around WAIS, the Brunt, the Bellingshausen Sea –

He looks up to see their baffled faces.

CHRIS. I didn't get a word of that.

WILL. It was just an abstract –

JENKS. Will's used to a specialist audience; what he's saying,
essentially, is he knows about ice –

SARIKA. Colin, Will hardly needs you –

CHRIS. Actually I rather think he does.

The thing is, Will, we're not working for the Government of
the Antarctic, even if we do have duty of care to the Falkland
Islands. Tessa and I are the servants of the Crown, we answer
to the people of Britain.

And while you were engaged in your research they voted us
in and now one of our largest and most venerable cities has
suffered a flood with how many casualties – ?

TESSA. Thirty-five, including a helicopter pilot brought down
in high winds, a shopkeeper knifed in an act of looting, a
whole floor of a care home drowned in their sleep.

CHRIS. How do you bloody retain all this, Tessa?

TESSA. I'm a woman, Christopher.

CHRIS. Right. Well. Good for you.

TESSA. I talked to everyone, the emergency services, the victims,
meteorologists, and not one of them mentioned the South Pole.

SARIKA. If I can speak for Will – to contextualise.

TESSA. Oh, so you know the context as well?

SARIKA. Because, okay, I visited Will and his team.

TESSA. Nice junket, on the taxpayer I expect.

SARIKA. Auditing research financed by the taxpayer. And
Will's work is, I think it's fair to say, Colin, groundbreaking
– am I right?

JENKS. He's a very brilliant scientist.

SARIKA. I mean, what Will's been saying is, yes, there are
massively accelerated melt-rates in the Arctic, but that we

tend to assume the Antarctic is stable. There's even a hypothesis, asserting its stability.

A hypothesis established by Colin, in fact. Maybe we cling to this because to believe otherwise is simply too terrifying.

JENKS. We cling to it because it has never been disproved.

SARIKA. But if all the ice in Antarctica were to melt –

JENKS. Inconceivable, actually –

SARIKA. – sea levels would rise –

WILL. Sixty metres.

JENKS. Oh, this is silly speculation.

WILL. Minimum.

CHRIS. Hang on a minute – how high's Nelson's Column?

WILL. Sorry?

CHRIS. To put this in perspective, how high's Nelson's Column?

JENKS. Oh. Fifty metres?

WILL. At five metres over sea level.

CHRIS. High enough for the old boy to see the sea.

JENKS. Will, you know I am not in any way sceptical about the risks, the risks are huge –

CHRIS. So, we might get Nelson if not the actual Column?

WILL. Okay, you may know about the Larsen B – here, okay, it's in your pack, the images –

JENKS. Mislabelled actually, I think.

SARIKA. What?

JENKS. And there's another dodgy caption saying this is the West Antarctic Ice Sheet when it's self evidently the Brunt.

CHRIS. In here?

SARIKA. My, my mistake.

TESSA. Where is that?

JENKS. Page ten.

TESSA. I see.

SARIKA. In fact I corrected it after Will's comments.

TESSA. Oh, so he's seen this too? I thought this was just an internal thing, Chris…?

CHRIS. It is.

Pause.

WILL. So. If I can go on. So. Ice is basically parked water; the Larsen B parked five-thousand-billion tonnes of it, and it went eight years ago, in two days, an ice shelf that held good for what –

JENKS. Twelve thousand years.

WILL. Thank you.

JENKS. It's where I cut my teeth.

WILL. So that's two-thousand-five-hundred-odd square miles of ice gone. Overnight.

JENKS. Interestingly enough with no discernible effect on sea level as yet. And I think largely a naturally occurring event.

CHRIS. But this is thousands of miles from us.

WILL. If you pour water in the bath it doesn't stay under the tap, Minister; the equilibrium of the ocean, of all oceans everywhere is disrupted. I work on the West Antarctic Ice Sheet, compared with which the Larsen's a pocket handkerchief. And the conventional wisdom, with one notable exception, is that its sheer bulk makes it immune to temperature rises, even when they are rising faster in the Antarctic than anywhere else on the planet –

JENKS. That conclusion is sound.

It would take centuries and unimaginable hikes in temperature to dismember an ice sheet of that scale and you know it!

WILL. Our studies suggest otherwise.

CHRIS. Look, this is terribly interesting but I fail to see the direct pertinence –

WILL. If the WAIS goes that's five metres sea-level rise minimum.

TESSA. Five metres?

WILL. Yes.

CHRIS. Five? Well, that sounds doable.

WILL *pulls out a large fold-out topographic map of the British Isles*.

WILL. 'Doable'! Okay, fine, let's look at who's affected by sea-level rises of just one metre. Avonmouth and right up the Severn; Tewksbury, Upton, Bridgnorth.

Wales, mainly South Wales –

CHRIS. Welsh Assembly.

TESSA. They can't vote that one away.

WILL. Well, Cardiff, yes, but otherwise Wales is –

TESSA. Serve 'em right for siting the Parliament by the docks.

WILL. The Dee. Liverpool. Chester, Runcorn.

JENKS. Ireland would form a barrier.

WILL. Barrow. Carlisle – Galloway –

CHRIS. Scottish Assembly. Not our problem.

TESSA. The case for devolution made.

JENKS. Can't we just extrapolate from there?

CHRIS. Let's see the whole picture.

TESSA. If there's any foundation for it.

CHRIS. You need to see if any of these county councils have begun preparation.

SARIKA. They haven't.

TESSA. Probably all Lib Dems.

CHRIS. Keep going! It's a bit like that programme, what is it, *Coast*.

TESSA. Oh, Christopher, you're incorrigibly middle-brow.

CHRIS. My girls like it!

WILL. The east is the most vulnerable.

Newcastle and above up to Berwick.

Hull, obviously. Whitby –

JENKS. Whitby's got fifty-metre cliffs.

WILL. Highly eroded.

TESSA. They can have Lincolnshire.

CHRIS. You're from Lincolnshire?

TESSA. Rugby.

CHRIS. Sarika's from there.

TESSA. I know. I recognise the accent. The nearest coastal resort was Skegness. Which my mother considered the perfect setting for our mandatory fortnight of cold picnics of potted meats in the dunes, returning home whiter than we left.

CHRIS. An intriguing image.

TESSA. Let it be consumed by the waves.

WILL. In due course it will be.

Then we reach the most vulnerable area of all. East Anglia.

TESSA. Fine! Set it loose from its moorings.

Let the land east of Peterborough float free.

CHRIS. Why exclude Peterborough?

They laugh.

WILL. Right. As someone whose parents live on the Norfolk coast I find it hard to share your insouciance. But okay, if you want me to stop there...

JENKS. Go on. You haven't reached London.

WILL. No. That's right, I haven't.

JENKS. Might as well go for the burn.

TESSA. London's got a wonderfully sizeable sluice gate on it. I've inspected it myself. Magnificent.

JENKS. Set to brook anything up to eight metres.

CHRIS. Can we go back to Norfolk?

WILL. Norfolk. Sure.

CHRIS. Just that we have this lovely flint cottage Holt way –

TESSA. Careful, Christopher – second homes can be a liability –

CHRIS. Just a family home. Nothing posh.

You're saying Norfolk's in the frame?

JENKS. Your home will be fine, minister.

London will be absolutely fine – this, this is all absurd.

WILL. You reckon London's safe?

TESSA. The chap at the Barrier told me himself.

WILL. So you think eight-metre waves are an impossibility?

TESSA. He certainly did.

WILL. So what about, say, 1953?

CHRIS. The coronation? Is that absolutely relevant?

WILL. The flood. Of 1953.

JENKS. '53 never got beyond five metres, Will.

WILL. With sea levels half a metre lower!

CHRIS. Even so.

WILL. Minister –

CHRIS. Chris.

WILL. Chris, 1953 was about a conjunction of circumstances. If it happened again, and I believe it is a question of when not if, it will be worse, far worse.

A perfect storm, say.

Sea level swollen from polar melt, warming and shifting currents, more vociferous storm surges, faster winds, higher tides – imagine that cold water rushing south east from Greenland, a great riptide blown and sucked and tugged across the Atlantic, gathering momentum as it goes, a mass of waters and turbulence, nothing forming an obstacle from Iceland to the Shetlands where high cliffs push it east like a ball flipped on a pinball machine, angering it further, and now, look, funnelled into the gap between the continent and the east coast, and my God, it's really ferocious now, and this is a spring tide, the sun and moon exerting their pull, sucking the currents into this great tower of water, down, down the eastern coast, smack into the rump of East Anglia and, yes, almost in reaction, sucked up the Thames Estuary and, yes, the Barrier may work, it may just work, but it may not and if, if the calculation made in a world of steady-state ocean patterns proves false then here it comes, up the Thames, and the Barrier proves as much a folly as the Maginot Line, and – well.

Pause.

CHRIS. We can't be much higher than sea level here. I mean, this is all reclaimed marsh.

TESSA. There's the embankment.

JENKS. It wouldn't be high enough to –

WILL. It enrages and funnels up the –

SARIKA. The Met's at the same level.

TESSA. The fire department.

CHRIS. The whole of Whitehall.

TESSA. And the Tube…

WILL. Absolutely. The whole sewage system –

CHRIS. Oh dear.

Pause.

I wonder if we're shutting the stable door after the thingy's –

SARIKA. The horse has –

CHRIS. Thank you.

Pause.

JENKS. At the risk of sounding pompous, I would suggest Will is being irresponsible.

WILL. Okay.

CHRIS. He seems to have done his homework.

JENKS. By training he's a glaciologist.

WILL. I'm a physicist actually.

JENKS. But you're no oceanologist, are you?

WILL. The boundaries between disciplines are pretty meaningless on this.

JENKS. Yeah, I know what you're saying but I think Chris and Tessa are entitled to know where you're coming from.

WILL. I was invited here –

JENKS. You see, that surprised me, Sarika.

I don't mean to pull rank, but if Chris wanted a second opinion, I happen to know everyone, everyone working on climate, working on ice, working on impacts –

CHRIS. We know you're well connected –

JENKS. I don't like to blow my own trumpet but as someone with five years in the office of Chief Scientific Advisor, as chair of the panel at the IPCC –

TESSA. Acronym –

SARIKA. Intergovernmental Panel on Climate Change –

WILL. Yeah, who I happen to think are truly criminally irresponsible –

JENKS. Really! 'Criminally irresponsible'?

The combined endeavours of the most respected researchers in the world?

WILL. By the time they finish the reading, the data's historical. This field shifts daily.

JENKS. They go through a rigorous review programme which I do not see here!

WILL. The world sends off its boffins, at five-year intervals, kicks the question into touch and takes the best-case scenario –

JENKS. Okay, okay. Gloves off. Chris, you and I, we're getting used to each other. As you know, as everyone knows, I was with the old regime. There's always a temptation to get in one's own people. I understand that temptation and I respect you for not giving way to it. Thus far. And what Will did here could be seen as useful – I don't happen to think he's right, I think he woefully overstates his case, I recognise the father in the son if you don't mind me saying, but, okay, we need to see the whole spectrum – and this, finally, is not about politics, it's about survival. I mean, what can a Conservative or Labour position on the weather actually meaningfully be? For or against? Sarika and I and your predecessor, who had his flaws, worked hard to draw up this review and until now, until your Government, we were nodded on and batted away and things moved too slowly but they were moving in the correct direction – and now with you and Tessa in one ministry this balance between slow, deep change and tooling up for what might ensue is being struck. Truly, we have an international process, we have the mechanisms and now we need to educate our people, roll out programmes for resilience – but above all else what we mustn't do now is panic. We need to stay cool, maintain our judgement. And Will here is offering panic not judgement.

TESSA. Colin's right. Let's confirm Sarika's paper, which is well argued, and which is meticulously researched – and, Colin, you had a large part to play in that – and let's get a large injection of cash into Civil Contingency, sign off on

this and go to the House and the press and get to work. What do you think, Chris?

CHRIS. What do I think?

Pause.

TESSA. We can't concern ourselves with this level of speculation. And we have here something we can agree on. Right?

You and I can go to David and... the work can begin.

JENKS. And, okay, perhaps Will could contribute to a wider brainstorming group – his contribution would be welcome...

TESSA. Of course, absolutely – in that context.

SARIKA. Well. I mean, I could strengthen the section on –

WILL. Sar...

SARIKA. On the ice-melt, say – Dr Paxton!

TESSA. Indeed, incorporate his research, why not? So. Chris?

CHRIS. What?

TESSA. Shall we sign off on – and go...?

CHRIS. No. I don't think so. No.

TESSA. No?

CHRIS. Yes. No.

TESSA. May I ask why?

CHRIS. I'm not prepared to be the minister who consigned Nelson's Column to the North Sea.

Pause.

TESSA. Christopher, nobody here truly believes that Nelson or indeed his column are in any danger of getting even the tiniest bit damp from the North Sea or any other body of water within the next millennium – isn't that so, Colin?

JENKS. Look, at worst, the IPCC are talking about half a metre sea-level rise and this is by 2100.

CHRIS. But Will here says they're out of date. Don't you?

WILL. Yes.

CHRIS. And this guy's out there, getting face time with the ice.

WILL. Which is melting exponentially.

CHRIS. And I don't much trust committees either, I certainly don't trust acronyms much, and I never ever take my bearings from anything intergovernmental.

JENKS. The cream of world science!

CHRIS. Anyway, Colin, when were you last where the data is?

JENKS. I think I have earned my spurs.

Ten years in the field.

SARIKA. But Will's just back from the Antarctic.

TESSA. And I'm just back from Alfreton.

My constituency. And climate change troubles the people of Alfreton a lot less than negative equity, defaulting banks and pre-teens defecating on their lawns. And whatever climate change might mean for us, and I don't pretend to know, we are not actually in Dhakar, we are in England and perhaps in that context we should be talking opportunity rather than disaster. A heaven-sent opportunity to change our ways, say, for mothers to get cooking again rather than stuffing ready-meals in their corpulent offspring –

CHRIS. Tessa, please –

TESSA. – an opportunity to galvanise work-shy teenagers to clear their drains, plant trees and dig gardens rather than going boss-eyed on Xbox –

CHRIS. Now, come on–

TESSA. I mean, if you want answers to this crisis talk to our senior citizens, look back not forty years, to how we bought and thought and how we lived then, caring for our homes and staying put with our families and jobs, then, then we were self-reliant and if climate change helps us recover that resilience it'll have done us a heck of a favour. I think.

CHRIS. I hardly think climate change should be treated as a pretext to turn this country into the Isle of Man.

WILL *is laughing*.

SARIKA. Will!

TESSA. I don't think I said anything funny!

WILL. I'm sorry, you actually seem to think this is a sort of, what, divine judgement?

TESSA. No. I see it as a test.

A test of our mettle.

And so far we're failing, aren't we?

JENKS. Mmm.

TESSA. Colin?

JENKS. I find it odd that somehow because I counsel caution, somehow I am considered to be diminishing the threat of anthropogenic climate change when I've been arguing all my adult life –

WILL. What, all your adult life?

JENKS. What's that?

SARIKA. Will –

JENKS. I'd like to know what you're driving at.

CHRIS. Guys, come on, let's set aside rivalries –

WILL. I just think you've got a track record of getting it wrong.

JENKS. What did you say?

SARIKA. He didn't mean that. Will, withdraw –

TESSA. Professor Jenks is universally admired –

WILL. Know where I was last week, Colin?

JENKS. I've no idea.

WILL. Pine Island Glacier.

Do you remember it?

JENKS. Of course I remember it.

WILL. This time last week.

JENKS. I expect the others are wondering what this is about. I know I am.

WILL. What it's about is over thirty wasted years.

SARIKA. Will, please, this is not the place –

CHRIS. Do we need time out, gentlemen?

JENKS. It's not complicated. Will's father was a brilliant –

WILL. 'Is' actually – still very much alive –

JENKS. Is a brilliant but retired glaciologist –

WILL. Retired!

JENKS. I suppose what this is about is how you want your science, ministers – I mean, do you want it intuitive, passionate, engaged but deeply flawed; or do you want it methodical, exacting and by extension a little slower.

WILL. I'm sorry, I can't listen to this –

SARIKA. Will's anger is grounded in his perception –

TESSA. I really don't like the way she seems primed to speak for him. Do you, Chris?

CHRIS. No. No, I don't like it much.

SARIKA. You ought to know the background.

JENKS. If we're going over the ancient past let me give you the full story at least.

I worked with Will's father. I was part of his team. In the Antarctic. 1970–'74.

A minor, eccentric scientific province then. A graveyard for ambition. You went for the penguins or to get away from your wife. I doubt Ted Heath would have given two hoots about us.

And Will's dad, a nice man, a good man –

WILL. He was your superior in every respect.

JENKS. I'm saying this as nicely as I can.

You actually weren't there.

You weren't born.

Have you ever considered he might not have told you the whole story –

Look, this is fruitless, I – I am happy to resign, I honestly don't think you need the two of us –

CHRIS. Finish your story, Colin.

WILL. Dad noticed oddities in ice movements, melt-rates.

JENKS. Explicable oddities.

WILL. Unprecedented motions.

JENKS. He made a leap from that –

WILL. He observed warming –

JENKS. No, there really was no pattern –

WILL. Three years of data actually!

JENKS. No, this was the thing, the data was contingent, localised –

WILL. And, he, Dad, extrapolated –

JENKS. He wanted to rush, recklessly, into print.

Shooting his mouth off, rushing into unproveable ideas of climate change –

WILL. He didn't call it climate change, no –

But he was silenced just the same.

JENKS. Silenced?

WILL. Silenced. Just as the facts were silenced.

Silenced by his colleague. By his friend.

By you. Because for you the time is never right to tell the truth.

JENKS. That is an utterly outrageous accusation – okay. Fine. This is difficult for you, Will. And for the lay audience. Okay. Imagine if a monk, say, in the medieval warming period had suggested the unduly hot summers were caused by spots on the sun, do you imagine he'd've got a sympathetic hearing? They'd have burned the bugger at the stake, wouldn't they? Or okay, let's say, if Newton had speculated on the theory of relativity in 1705, do you think the Royal Society would have said, 'Crikey, interesting stuff, Sir Isaac'? They'd have branded the man insane.

WILL. This has absolutely no relevance to you and my dad, none.

JENKS. An idea needs its time!

Back then the time was not ripe. No one was talking about global warming, no one. In some areas the sea was cooling.

Ice was being added. The ice sheet was stable, is stable, remains stable.

Your father, yes, perhaps, just perhaps, now we may consider him right, okay, but then, I'm sorry, he was utterly wrong. Because the time was not ripe.

WILL. For you it never is. Until it's too late.

JENKS *starts gathering up his things.*

JENKS. I really shouldn't have to account here for taking to task bad science.

I have argued all my working life that method is as significant as result.

CHRIS. Colin, don't –

JENKS. I'll be honest, whilst I don't approve of this Government, I came here today with an open mind but I am bound to say if you are set on destabilising the vital work achieved so far and thereby endangering years of work on mitigation – which in the end, William, is the only way, the only way to prevent this planet from becoming entirely hostile to life – then I will have to make public this outrageous – coup –

CHRIS. Now you're being petulant.

JENKS. I like that! You invite me in –

CHRIS. Did we invite you in?

SARIKA. No.

TESSA. Yes.

JENKS. So it gets ever shabbier. Look, it's fine.

Have your fresh face. I think in many respects his urgency
will serve you well. He's clearly more malleable than I ever
was. But the thing about this is if you get it wrong, if you
back the wrong boy, my God there will be grave
implications. Ask Will's father – science can be unforgiving,
especially when the stakes are this high.

CHRIS. Do you know what, Colin, you are a very arrogant man.

JENKS. Oh, what I am is neither here nor there.

CHRIS. I have to answer for what I do to the people of Britain.

JENKS. And I have to answer to the planet.

Unfortunately it doesn't get to vote.

He goes.

TESSA. Chris, I think we should have a talk.

CHRIS. Fine.

TESSA. I mean – alone.

CHRIS. We need to get on.

TESSA. How can we proceed now?

CHRIS. We have to get on.

TESSA. You can't draw up a policy without the backing of
experienced scientific advice.

CHRIS. We have experienced scientific advice.

TESSA. I don't want to be rude but I wonder if William here
has any idea about... policy.

CHRIS. I think that is pretty damn rude.

Will?

Pause.

WILL. It's true I am a data rather than an ideas man.

SARIKA. You have ideas.

WILL. I slightly don't trust policy.

CHRIS. Well, if you don't mind me saying, that's not much fucking use, is it.

Pause.

TESSA. Let me go and talk Colin down. Chris.

CHRIS. Sorry. Sorry. But no. He is the problem. We don't need him.

TESSA. No, I really think this is unwise now.

CHRIS. Well, this is my ministry, finally.

TESSA. I think we should run it past David.

CHRIS. And David is my oldest dearest friend.

TESSA. Who asked me to feed back on today.

On the decisions, today.

Pause.

CHRIS. I see.

TESSA. So let me fetch Colin.

CHRIS. No. Fuck him. And, okay, fuck David.

TESSA. We aren't alone, Christopher.

CHRIS. So what do we do, Will?

I mean, you say the international process is, what, too slow?

WILL. I'd say it was glacial. But actually these days the glaciers move faster.

CHRIS. Very good but what replaces it?

WILL. I don't know what the levers of –

CHRIS. What would you say to the people of Britain tomorrow? Because tomorrow at seven I am on *Today*, Sarika will be getting our briefing out by five to all the major political hacks, I will fly to Bristol and launch our policy, I have to go to David and show how we might divvy out the largesse we've been granted and do you know what I can't say the world's about to end, and there's fuck all we can do about it. Do you see where I'm coming from?

Pause.

WILL. You want my ideas?

TESSA. Don't be a little tease.

WILL. Okay. Yes. I do have ideas.

CHRIS. Well?

WILL. An immediate massive injection of cash into flood defences.

Barrages, sluice gates, groins.

Sea walls. On all rivers. All estuaries.

An arm cradled around the nation.

On an infinitely larger scale than the Thames Barrier. Levees, polders, houses on stilts. A constant state of readiness for evacuation of all coastal settlements.

Indeed all riverine settlements.

And all this by the end of summer.

CHRIS. What, all –

And – evacuate – to, to – to where?

WILL. I have no idea.

CHRIS. Have you any idea of the cost?

WILL. No.

CHRIS. Not least the social cost?

Pause.

TESSA. This is – ridiculous.

CHRIS. Tessa, you will look as much of cunt as me if you don't get behind this.

TESSA. Don't you ever use that word in conjunction with me ever again.

Pause.

SARIKA. But what of the long term?

WILL. Compulsory purchase of inland areas.

Demolish all houses that are not carbon neutral. Convert all of East Anglia to wetland as a protective sump. Carbon rationing universally applied. One car per street. Cease road construction, in fact begin to close roads. Gear all farming land to local food production and move towards zero imports. Restructure the economy to local goods and services. Turn schools into centres for resilience-building.

Is this what you're looking for?

Pause.

CHRIS. How could we do – any of this?

I mean, even in wartime –

SARIKA. But this is a war. Isn't it?

CHRIS. Against what?

SARIKA. Because this is about defending our people.

TESSA. Yes. Against themselves. Their worst selves.

CHRIS. Okay. Go on.

WILL. That's it.

CHRIS. That's it?

WILL. It has to be as simple and as radical as that.

CHRIS. Right.

Pause.

TESSA. 'Let no man say this may not be done.'

Franklin Delano Roosevelt.

CHRIS. 'Let no man say this may not be done.'

TESSA. We did it before. The last war.

Nearly one hundred per cent drop in car use, one hundred per cent rise in agricultural production, malnutrition abolished! Within five years. In the middle of a war. This, this is the resilience we're talking about, surely.

'Let no man say this may not be done!'

They stand in silence. Suddenly a phone starts ringing.

SARIKA. That shouldn't be ringing.

CHRIS. Why not?

SARIKA. It's only for when, for if the lines are down.

CHRIS. Let it ring off.

TESSA. No. Answer it.

CHRIS. We're meant to be incommunicado here.

SARIKA. It'll stop. It's sure to stop.

It doesn't.

CHRIS. Look, I'll answer it.

TESSA. No, I'll – maybe it's David?

CHRIS. Let me –

SARIKA. It's okay. I'll put it on conference.

She does.

Hello?

An eerie sound of breathing and then a giggle.

Who is this? Hello?

Suddenly we hear children singing 'Happy Birthday'.

CHRIS*'s eyes fill with tears.*

CHRIS. Oh. Thank you, guys. Thank you.

He turns to WILL.

Thank you.

Blackout.

End of Act One.

ACT TWO

Scene One

The same, September that year. It's eight o'clock on Saturday evening. WILL is alone. He's wearing an identity card around his neck and a suit which is ill-fitting. He looks tired. He's on the phone.

WILL. Oh. Yes. I need an external...

Will Paxton, yes, the advisor, the Chief Government – I don't need to clear it.

Just take the number, please.

Okay. 01485 792264. Yep.

I can wait. Yep.

TESSA enters. She unpacks her flask and picks up one of the dossiers. WILL smiles at her.

TESSA. This line is not for private calls.

WILL. I know. Sorry.

TESSA. These lines have to be kept free at all times.

WILL. It's my parents.

You see they live, they're on the other side of the Wash. From Skegness. Right, right on the shore, literally. In the path.

Pause.

Okay, I'll leave a message.

Dad, Mum. If you're there.

It's Will. If you're there, well, you need to get out. I know, I know you think I have... compromised myself. I know I am, yes, *persona non grata*. I know.

But I am, okay, I'm fearful for you.

That's it. Get right out. Right now.

And, please call. Call the ministry.

Please.

He replaces the phone.

TESSA. Is 996 unusually high or low?

WILL. Sorry?

TESSA. 996 millibars? Unusually high or low?

WILL. Low. Well, perhaps not unusually low, well, quite –

TESSA. Not unusually?

WILL. Sorry, where's this?

TESSA. But low would not be good?

WILL. Well, in itself, no, low is fine.

TESSA. But in this situation?

WILL. No, in this situation low is bad, very bad.

TESSA. But 996 millibars is not unusually low?

WILL. It depends – and actually – look, here –

He checks his laptop.

See. East of Berwick it's 980.

TESSA. Out at sea? Don't we need it shockingly low over land?

WILL. I don't know about need.

TESSA. Shouldn't the wind be incredibly strong?

WILL. Yes. Wind direction and, yes, the strength is the critical
thing.

*He settles down to factor information in to his model. She
watches.*

Weather station at Flamborough says, what, force nine.

TESSA. Force nine's not exceptional.

WILL. Seven-metre waves. Sixty mph, maybe seventy.

TESSA. So, winds rising to force ten, possibly.

Sounds better.

WILL. As it makes landfall it'll hit power lines.

TESSA. Good. Extensive property damage?

WILL. Almost certainly.

TESSA. Trees down, roads blocked?

WILL. Trees, vegetation, I mean, that's... serious.

The unknown is surge impact. Positive or negative.

TESSA. Surging... water?

WILL. We'll know when it hits, well, Skegness.

TESSA. Which is likely to be when?

WILL. Within the next forty minutes.

Cleethorpes or Mablethorpe'll indicate what we're in for.

Get there in, what... ten minutes.

Pause.

TESSA. You'd make a good weather forecaster. They're so ingratiating nowadays. I heard one chap warning us to look out for 'lots of the wet stuff'. 'The wet stuff'! You wouldn't have thought it possible to dumb down the weather forecast.

So easterly winds, very low pressure, very high tides and a potential – surge?

WILL. Positive surge.

TESSA. Which is good?

WILL. Bad. Negative is away from the shore, positive is –

If we're lucky it'll be negative.

TESSA. If it's negative we're in trouble.

The phone rings.

That'll be Gold Command in Mablethorpe.

Yes. Due to call in, yes, about now.

To initiate procedures. With our blessing.

WILL. Well, go ahead.

TESSA. I thought you'd say that.

But what if I do and nothing transpires?

WILL. That's a risk worth taking, Minister.

In '53 they missed the signals.

Hundreds of lives were lost.

TESSA *answers the phone.*

TESSA. Tessa Fortnum. What are the conditions with you? Uh-huh. But it is windy.

Sorry, your patch is – what's your judgement?

Hang on.

(*To* WILL.) Heavy winds, high seas, as yet no imminent indication of inundation.

(*On phone.*) We need a minute's further consultation. Yes.

She hangs up. Pause.

It doesn't seem to be happening, does it?

WILL. Well – it may not happen.

TESSA. What makes you so sure it will?

WILL. There are indications that the North Atlantic has taken on unprecedented volumes of meltwater even within the week.

Everyone's operating with the idea of a steady-state sea level. The Met Office haven't changed their models. But I cannot see how with the loss of a third of Greenland's ice this summer we won't get at least a metre increase in wave height right across the board.

TESSA. But we see no evidence of that yet.

WILL. Because of localised conditions.

TESSA. Weasel words.

WILL. Conditions will vary enormously –

TESSA. Weasel words, Will.

WILL. Minister, it's the local that kills you in the end.

Pause. TESSA unzips a dossier and pulls out a piece of paper. She slides it to WILL.

I'm sorry. What's this?

TESSA. Read it.

He does.

Sign it.

WILL. Hang on –

TESSA. Sign it before they call back.

WILL. But what's the significance of this?

TESSA. Simply clarifies the precise nature of your advice.

WILL. But what does it bind me into?

TESSA. It simply states that at the time of the decision to evacuate you offered the best scientific advice available. And that in the event of any subsequent inquiry you will account for that advice.

WILL. So it's letting you off the hook?

TESSA. Making the hook fit for purpose.

The phone rings again.

WILL. Well, wouldn't that be taken as read anyway?

TESSA. These are exceptional circumstances.

This is an unminuted meeting.

No Civil Servants present.

Yes, these are extraordinary circumstances.

If you sign this, I will proceed and lives may indeed be saved.

WILL. Is that what it takes to save a life round here?

TESSA. That's what it takes.

WILL looks at her; seizes a pen, signs; she picks up the phone.

Hello. Yes.

Our information is that you should proceed –

Yes. Concentrate on the waterfront. You've commandeered community centres? Yes, you have authorisation to appropriate all forms of public transport. Shut down all incoming roads and make dual carriageways westbound only.

What? If it's at all possible, keep all power stations running. Secure, let me see, secure electricity substations, err, all localised media outlets broadcast the given message.

We want quarter-hourly reports here.

Good luck.

She hangs up.

Impenetrable East Yorkshire slur.

Did I acquit myself all right?

WILL. Very… authoritative.

She takes the paper from him and folds it, tucks it back in her dossier.

TESSA. I should put in an appearance down the corridor at Triple C. They'll want to know about London. A few pensioners in a leisure centre in Mablethorpe hardly merits the attention of the state. But shutting this city down, well… if you make the wrong call you won't be thanked, will you?

What should I say? At Triple C?

WILL. Oh, you're asking me?

TESSA. For advice, yes. You are an advisor, aren't you?

WILL. I think we go through Chris on that, don't we?

TESSA. Do you see him here?

I am acting head of this ministry.

In this blissful period of his absence I give the orders.

Has Sarika recalled him from his hols?

WILL. Why would I know that?

She smiles.

TESSA. Not that he's far away, only Dorset.

Having been advised to go low-carbon. Or was that your idea?

WILL. Sarika is quite independent from me.

TESSA. Hard to imagine Christopher in a tent.

Not that you need to now as he's on YouTube in Crocs and a cape.

One of the reasons I don't do holidays.

They expose you to ridicule.

So should we evacuate London and if so which boroughs?

WILL. That's not my call.

TESSA. But what's your hunch?

WILL. Let's see what the next thirty minutes brings us. See how the contingency plan fares.

She laughs.

TESSA. And how do you imagine it will fare, Will?

Oh, of course, you just said, on telly.

'Dangerous gimmicks rather than policy.'

Weren't we meant to say 'eye-catching initiatives'?

WILL. Yeah, half-baked crap like district councils competing for flood defences!

TESSA. We say: 'Rewarding the innovators.'

WILL. Setting Mablethorpe against Cleethorpes?

   What happens if I'm unlucky enough to live in Cleethorpes? Tough shit, I guess.

TESSA. We say: 'Resources must be husbanded.'

WILL. Great, self-financing disaster management!

TESSA. We say the market has to drive it.

WILL. So was the Great Wall of China self-financing?

   The Battle of Britain?

TESSA. Chris is adamant climate change won't be a Trojan horse for the nanny state.

WILL. What does the state exist for if not to protect us on nights like these?

TESSA. But am I right in thinking you signed numerous documents which stated you accept corporate responsibility?

   Do you think I am impressed with Christopher's shockingly inept tenure at his post? Do you think I haven't been appalled by the shoddy, half-baked improvisation that has passed for policy issuing from this ministry?

   Pause.

WILL. Right. No. Sorry.

   Pause.

TESSA. Think of tonight as a gift, Will. For you and me. The way forward is to pray for the worst.

WILL. I'm not especially given to prayer, Tessa.

TESSA. Do you know what I like about you, Will?

   You have fire in you and it burns hot. But what you learn from a lifetime in politics is to keep your powder dry. That sometimes we have to go to the bottom to get what we want. What you and I want is simply not conceivable in modern Britain. This is a consensual nation in the end. Only takes a

few loudmouths in a parish council meeting, a few mobilised truckers, an unusually dedicated journalist and the boldest of plans get scuppered. Because we're committed to something we call democracy, which in fact is simply the aggregate will of the greediest and most vocal. We know there's no half measures in the face of disaster, we know the half-done thing is worse than nothing at all because the half-done thing replaces actual action. You pointed that out to us. And what did that achieve exactly?

You'd think a lethal flood in Bristol might wake us up but we find we can live with it, muddle on through. Maybe we have to go through the fire to come out entirely changed.

So, yes, I say pray for your positive surge.

Her phone pings.

WILL. Is that Chris?

TESSA. That'd be telling. So. London?

Your best hunch.

WILL. Let's just see how Skegness fares first, shall we?

He picks up a phone. She packs her laptop, ready to go.

SARIKA enters with some pizzas.

SARIKA. Minister? Sorry, I thought you were in Triple C.

TESSA. Where were you?

SARIKA. Oh – trying to reach Chris –

TESSA. Until Christopher is in this room at that phone, you should be at my beck and call.

SARIKA. Well, if I may say, that's not –

TESSA. No, you may not say!

This is a crisis and procedure must be observed.

In your absence I authorised the evacuation of Mablethorpe. Now you need to monitor its progress.

She goes.

SARIKA. Thanks for sticking up for me.

WILL. Sorry. Hey.

He goes to kiss her, she flinches.

What? Why did you do that?

SARIKA. It's fine. Nothing. So how do you feel it went?

WILL. Oh. That. No. Came across as aggressive.

SARIKA. Aggressive? A little tense, perhaps. Understandably tense.

WILL. So you saw it?

SARIKA. The tail end.

WILL. They ask such dumb questions.

'Is this gonna be Katrina or worse than Katrina?'

SARIKA. That was a silly question, yes.

WILL. So you saw me, what could I say, I had to say your report's fallacious, your data's dated and I'm sorry I wasn't there to argue for the Government. Not simply that, anyway.

SARIKA. Not simply that, no.

WILL. I mean, I am independent, finally.

SARIKA. Well. Not – entirely, Will. No. You're not.

Only have three of these.

Embarrassingly from Pizza Hut.

Margheritas. Going cold.

WILL. There's a bit more at stake than the provenance of your fucking pizzas.

SARIKA. Right. I'm aware of that.

Look, maybe you should go back to the flat.

WILL. What?

SARIKA. You know, get a bit of sleep, rest up.

WILL. But I'm meant to be here, right.

SARIKA. Strictly speaking you're advisory not implementation.

WILL. Damn right I'm advisory and you need all the advice you can get.

SARIKA. There are teams of people below you now.

WILL. None of them has any urgency – why do you guys always love to defer?

SARIKA. What? Don't, don't start putting this on me.

WILL. No, I don't mean you – I mean, I dunno, this.

Pause, he dials again.

(*On phone.*) Yes. Me again. 01485 792264. Yep.

I can wait. Yep. Yes, as I said before, I am fucking authorised, thank you.

SARIKA. Will!

You didn't reach them earlier?

WILL. Not answering my calls, blanking my e-mails, thought Mum was thawing a bit, but it's clearly total war now.

SARIKA. They won't do anything stupid.

WILL. Yeah – what about Dad's novel take on sea defences? 'Let the sea prevail!' Tonight's the night for that.

SARIKA. That wasn't serious, Will, that was bravado.

WILL. Oh, you don't know Dad.

He plays a long, long game.

SARIKA. They've left the house.

Not answering confirms that.

I mean, Jenny could have sent me, at the very least, a text.

WILL. I never fucking taught her to – to text.

Okay, message: Will again, really need to hear from you. Call Sarika – what's your number? Sar?

SARIKA. She knows it.

WILL. Say it again.

SARIKA. 07796 533745. When are you going to get a mobile?

He rings off irritably.

WILL. I need to go there.

SARIKA. What?

WILL. What am I doing here? I need to just go.

SARIKA. You're needed here.

WILL. You were just sending me back to the – yeah, I could get a train –

SARIKA. I need you here. They are fine, fine, fine.

Another phone rings, SARIKA *answers.*

Hello.

Who's that? Are you the Environment Agency?

Yes, I see, yes.

(*To* WILL.) Skegness want to know whether to initiate procedures.

WILL. Can we – in the absence of – ?

SARIKA (*on phone*). I think you should be on standby.

WILL. Tell them we can make a judgement –

SARIKA. We'll make a judgement in –

WILL. Fifteen –

SARIKA. Call again in fifteen – okay.

SARIKA gets a text message.

Ah. Great. Thank fuck. He's in.

WILL. Your absentee minister?

SARIKA. You prefer Lady Macbeth at the helm?

WILL. She takes the tough decisions.

SARIKA. Oh, yeah, she loves it. Tough, nasty, she thrives on it. You seem to like it too.

WILL. I admire her steadfastness.

SARIKA. Whatever goes wrong tonight she relishes, whatever goes right she profits from and if she profits it will be an unalloyed disaster.

Imagine a country run by Tessa?

I mean, it is not beyond the bounds –

WILL. She attends to the detail.

She's got guts and –

SARIKA. Every time you play her off against Chris, she is strengthened.

WILL. Chris's spent the summer back-pedalling, dithering, muddying.

SARIKA. Actually he's risked his neck for your thesis which seems, now –

WILL. Hang on! My thesis? Sarika?

SARIKA. Oh God, we don't have time for a – domestic. Got him for thirty then we're choppering him in to King's Lynn to meet the people of King's Lynn.

WILL. Should the people of King's Lynn be in King's Lynn right now?

SARIKA. Wants to go up and make the judgement himself –

WILL. The storm'll hit them in twenty minutes.

SARIKA. Well, then he can oversee the procedures.

Inspect the evacuation centre – in, let me see, Holkham Market.

WILL. There's no such place.

SARIKA. Yes, yes, there is, it's in Norfolk.

WILL. No, Holkham Market does not exist.

SARIKA. No, okay, fine, Swaffham Market –

WILL. No, not Swaffham, that's –

SARIKA. It has a bloody market in it somewhere.

WILL. Downham Market maybe?

SARIKA. Thank you, thank you, Downham Market.

WILL. But they shouldn't be there –

SARIKA. That's the specified evacuation centre –

WILL. No, they shouldn't be there –

SARIKA. It's, it's inland –

WILL. Less than ten metres over sea level.

SARIKA. It's fifteen miles inland, Will.

WILL. If the waves get as high as predicted, fifteen miles is
    nothing –

SARIKA. Oh, come on, the force of the –

WILL. Do you not believe me either?

SARIKA. Maybe you should start to speak in feasible terms –
    and we have to defer to the people on the ground. This is not
    the Kremlin, I am not Stalin.

WILL. Stalin knew how to move a population –

CHRIS *enters with a bottle of wine, in a kagool with a suit
    carrier and a pair of shoes; without noting* WILL, *he starts
    to strip to his pants and put on his formal gear.*

CHRIS. Isn't there something almost festive about a national
    catastrophe?

All the trivial bullshit gone.

The thin veneer of civilisation stripped away. After a
fortnight under canvas I'm braced for anything.

Raining when we pegged the bugger out, so much I spent the
entire day in a cape and swimmers, only to be filmed by my
kids, which you can take a gander at on YouTube if you like.

I would hazard a guess you've not woken up at 3 a.m. afloat on a groundsheet, guy-ropes flagellating your face – I tell you, it tests the resilience of family life to absolute breaking point.

That pizza going begging?

SARIKA. That's for you.

CHRIS. Is this the best you can do?

Fucking Pizza Hut. Jesus Christ.

SARIKA. I know, I'm sorry.

CHRIS. I bet Ed Miliband didn't have to chew on Pizza Hut.

TESSA *enters*.

SARIKA. Tessa. Pizza?

TESSA. Christopher.

CHRIS. Yeah. Surprised?

TESSA. You made it back.

CHRIS. Is that a problem for you?

TESSA. I don't see why it would be.

SARIKA. Pizza, Tessa?

Margherita or margherita?

TESSA. I'm gluten-intolerant.

CHRIS *eats his pizza messily. A pause*.

CHRIS. How've you found the stewardship, Tessa?

TESSA. Oh. Vexed. Of course.

CHRIS. 'Vexed'! I hear you've been decisive.

TESSA. I took advice.

CHRIS. What, from Disaster Tsar here?

WILL. Don't.

TESSA. You were incommunicado.

CHRIS. I was in Corfe Castle. In high fucking winds. Doing my low-carbon duty.

I've been on the phone since we hit London. Don't recall any probings, any consultations.

WILL. The conditions merited action.

CHRIS. Oh! Hello, Nostradamus.

Pleased with your telly debut?

WILL. You saw it?

CHRIS. Caught the highlights on the phone.

WILL. Right.

SARIKA. Shall we move on from that?

CHRIS. Might have been helpful to have some of your more critical thoughts in advance.

WILL. I have expressed my doubts, I think.

CHRIS. Productively. Until now.

WILL. I don't think I ever suggested I was going to be some vehicle for Government propaganda.

CHRIS. 'Propaganda.' My word!

For a scientist, you're somewhat given to histrionics, aren't you.

WILL. If you want me to step down I will step down because clearly in your eyes –

CHRIS. Okay, why don't you just do that?

In the middle of your longed-for national disaster, sure, just walk out.

Why not? Not your problem, right?

WILL. Look, if I have aired valid questions about the many, many shortcomings of your handling of –

CHRIS. Do you actually have any concept of duty? Do you?

WILL. To what?

CHRIS. 'To what?' To your country, perhaps.

SARIKA. Chris.

CHRIS. Maybe you think you're a citizen of Antarctica?

Maybe you think we're governing an iceberg and a couple of emperor penguins here?

WILL. This sort of insouciance, on tonight of all nights, is frankly –

CHRIS. He thinks we're insouciant!

Doesn't even realise we're scared to death. 'Cos we took a punt on you, Will.

WILL. You think I'm making all this up? Have you seen the footage of the waves? We've never seen waves this size in our coastal waters. Look, look. Here, this is a webcam, off Spurn Head.

CHRIS. Waves that, as I understand, are set to remain out at sea. Where they belong.

But, Tessa, I hear you took the initiative on Lincolnshire.

TESSA. Yes. Mablethorpe at least.

CHRIS. Oh, and apparently it's a bloody mess.

TESSA. Is it?

CHRIS. Oh, yeah. One A-road –

SARIKA. A1031.

CHRIS. Thank you. Log-jammed in all lanes.

Same on the coastal roads.

Emergency services in a blind funk.

When they get out of it and the sea stays offshore, boy, are they gonna be pissed off at – well, at you.

So who's next in line for the implementation of the plan. Sarika?

SARIKA. Regionally: Norfolk. Suffolk. Essex. Then London.

CHRIS. All of London? Should have thought Muswell Hill
could sit tight.

SARIKA. All riverine boroughs.

CHRIS. 'All riverine boroughs'?

TESSA. It's a difficult call, Chris.

You weren't here to make it.

CHRIS. Yes. Yes, it is a difficult call.

He sits down and eats more pizza.

Government's a bitch, isn't it?

You deregulate the banks and they melt down. You regulate
them, they haemorrhage capital. Light touch, they fuck up;
heavy hand, they fuck up.

Oh, by the way, Tessa, David asked me to assert overall
control.

TESSA. When?

CHRIS. When? I don't have to tell you when.

TESSA. I see.

CHRIS (*to* WILL). So, Einstein. Waves but no floods?

WILL. The surge and tendency is increasingly –

CHRIS. I said, no floods as yet?

WILL. As yet? No.

CHRIS. The promised deluge failed to deluge? Noah's ark still
in the dry dock?

WILL. We have to act on the precautionary principle.

CHRIS. When the cure is worse than the sickness, I'd say that's
arguable.

SARIKA. What are we going to do about London?

CHRIS. Do you know what, I have a plan!

We do nothing.

SARIKA. Nothing? No… evacuation.

TESSA. Think about this, Chris.

CHRIS. I have, thanks, Tessa.

It's Saturday night out there in one of the greatest cities in the world. Theatres are full of audiences, clubs, clubbers, lapdancers are making oligarchs cream in lapbars, kebabs being gobbled by the dozen, smokers in huddles outside riverside pubs; everyone's enjoying a moderately breezy night in September. The Met Office predict choppy seas and high winds. Life's going about its business. And in here we have Nostradamus telling us the sky's falling in.

WILL. You really have absorbed nothing.

CHRIS. You know what the Conservatives stand for? Small state, individual freedom, *laissez* fucking *faire* and British common sense.

TESSA. Well, we also stand for a strong state, moral governance and –

CHRIS. Would Nelson cack his pants because of high seas?

Nothing is what we are going to do.

Blitz fucking spirit.

'Above all else do no harm.'

Pause.

WILL. And – okay – what about – East Anglia?

CHRIS. You take a personal interest in that.

So do I.

WILL. You have property there.

CHRIS. Are you cheeking me?

WILL. Chris, whatever you think of me, seriously, you have got to give evacuation orders. It's the brave thing to do, it's the right thing to do, you need to do it. I have family –

CHRIS. What about Lincolnshire?

No juicy inundations there?

Nothing tsunami scale, just the odd bodyboarding breaker, right?

WILL. Yes, but it depends on the surge –

CHRIS. What are you talking about?

WILL. It depends on local tidal conditions, wind speed, direction, force of rain, err, sandbanks...

CHRIS. So many ungovernable factors!

David thinks evacuation is a mistake.

TESSA. What about Cleethorpes?

You said it would hit Cleethorpes.

WILL. Looks like, err, it didn't – looks like.

Looks like, as I understand it, the tidal surge worked against the worst of it.

Negative surge.

CHRIS. Oh, more surges now. You do learn a lot in this job.

WILL. It's just, it's the unpredictable element.

CHRIS. Do you know what's the unpredictable element? You, mate.

WILL. Minister, I understand it's complicated, I know it seems so frequently confusing and ambiguous but we are dealing with nature here –

CHRIS. What's the prognosis for Skeggie then?

WILL. Waves could be anything up to ten metres. High tide there too, so it's close in. I mean, I allow for increased sea level which the Met Office don't –

TESSA. Hang on. You're correcting the Met Office's figures now?

WILL. They're too low.

TESSA. But they use satellite images.

WILL. They're too low.

CHRIS *laughs*.

SARIKA. Will.

WILL. The Met Office don't factor higher sea levels in, they work on existing median wave height, but I predict –

CHRIS. I mean, is there anyone, anyone bar you in the right?

WILL. It's an adjustment up, it's not enormously significant. But if it's right, Skegness is going under.

TESSA. When? Exactly?

WILL. Ten minutes.

Pause. The phone rings.

That'll be them. Now.

Seeking authorisation.

CHRIS. Right. Feeling lucky, Tessa?

WILL. You need to answer it.

CHRIS. I'll be the judge of that.

The phone rings.

TESSA. Ever been to Skegness, Christopher?

CHRIS. I may be middle-brow but I'm not low-brow.

TESSA. Has its charms.

One long strand of beach.

Butlins. The Fairy Dell Swimming Pool. Not to mention Gibraltar Point.

Largest colony of lapwings in Britain.

WILL. You really need to answer that.

CHRIS. I'm a big fan of the lapwing.

Lovely bird.

The most eccentric flight patterns.

WILL. Okay, hang on, Mablethorpe seems…

TESSA. The waves seem to be –

SARIKA. Has it been – bypassed?

WILL. Yeah. Yes. Negative surge.

Please answer the phone.

CHRIS. Cleethorpes nil, Mablethorpe nil.

He answers the phone.

Christopher Casson.

Yes. Yes. I hear you.

Is the tide in? High winds?

What is your view on that?

Right. Right.

You sit tight. If circumstances change, of course, call in.
Remain on standby. (*He rings off.*) Sarika, I think it's only
fair if you do a ring-round confirming that, contrary to earlier
indications, Eastern England can curl up on the sofa in front
of *Strictly Come Dancing*.

SARIKA. Okay. You're sure.

CHRIS. What do you think?

WILL. You're making a terrible mistake.

She begins the call; her lines run through the following.

SARIKA. Okay, we need to alert the following to revert to
standby status.

Gold Command D: King's Lynn.

Gold Command E: Cromer.

Gold Command F: Yarmouth.

Gold Command G: Sizewell.

Gold Command H: Woodbridge.

Gold Command I: Walton-on-the-Naze.

CHRIS. Anyone fancy some wine?

He pours the wine into plastic cups.

TESSA. I have my punch, actually.

WILL watches the storm track forward on his laptop.

WILL. Sutton-on-Sea. Look. Very close in there, getting closer to land.

Chapel St Leonards. Maybe.

Ingoldmells in three minutes.

Wow – force eleven winds.

A dreamy silence.

TESSA. We'd travel a hundred miles on one of those filthy coaches and for a hundred miles nothing much changed at all, except the land became more and more featureless until finally it gave way to a featureless sea.

It just used to make me feel utterly… melancholy.

WILL. Okay. That's Ingoldmells. Right.

But they're at mid-tide so they should be… might be…

CHRIS. Listen to those names.

All the dreadful small places of England finally granted true pathos.

The smelly chip shops, the empty arcades full of kids high on alcopops – the listless promenades populated by potato-faced chavs. Whoosh!

WILL. Ingoldmells Point. Any minute… now.

CHRIS. Time to pop out for a piss then?

WILL. Okay, for years I was told by my father that our leaders, our representatives, were ignorant, self-interested, cynical, obsessed with their careers, their egos, indifferent to the truly great questions, immune to the drama of the natural world, innumerate, utterly shallow.

For a while I argued against that. I did.

Coming here, coming here was my response to what he said. I felt the stakes were too high, truly, to think what he thought. So I came here and I broke their hearts and that's my problem. But here, tonight, you've confirmed everything they said and not only that, you've made the charge sheet far, far longer. Because you're indolent. Because you're ignorant. Because you're totally fucking lethal.

CHRIS *chucks his wine in* WILL*'s face.*

CHRIS. It's official, Nostradamus. The sky remained firmly in the firmament.

High time you got back to your penguins. Okay, Tessa, we can take the rap for this debacle collectively.

TESSA. No, Christopher, it's perfectly clear I am squarely in the frame.

CHRIS. Well, that's very gracious of you. David might feel we both have to bear the brunt. Sarika? I guess, given you brought Dr Paxton into play, I think that might argue for re-deployment at the very least.

SARIKA. Okay. I am happy to offer my –

WILL. Oh my God. There it is. There it finally is.

TESSA. Positive?

WILL. Positive surge.

Suddenly all the phones ring at once; they listen, stunned; then each seizes their own handset; these next lines run together.

CHRIS. What? Yes, yes. I don't know who you are. Where, where are you calling from – where? Boston. Oh, Boston, Lincolnshire. Ah, Environment, Environment Agency. So it's hitting, what, we were expecting it later, a little later, but you say – there should, I presume there's a whole – I mean, clearly telecommunications are still holding – you're actually really hard to hear – you should have the emergency services to hand, yes, the idea was, the locality plan – how high?

Shit, yes, that's pretty bloody high – look, we – the plan is, the way it works is –

Yes, stay on the phone; okay, you have the utilities people there, it's crucial that we try and keep power in, keep roads clear –

TESSA. Yes, yes, it is, no, that's fine, no, I'm not but keep, keep talking, we were under the – under – can you actually hear me – that evacuation was underway in all vicinities – to, where, well, presumably to, I dunno, is it Sleaford, are you near – do you have –

You have the secured line but otherwise – are there any firefighters? Well, we can't mobilise the army all up and down the coast, clearly we need to save – Chris, the whole front, Chris, this is Skegness and the whole – Sarika, sorry to cut in – is it possible to calm down, I know, you need – you need – you need to calm down, you really need to calm right down –

WILL. Oh, right right right – sorry, can you see, can you say, could you estimate – you're where? Gibraltar Point, yes, I see it, hang on, my laptop battery, shit, it's run down, sorry, okay, is it possible to put a figure – on the size – of the – of course, of course you need to – but the wind speed, for instance – it would be incredibly helpful to put a figure – five metres? Shit, sorry, this is gone, yes. You think more? You'd say more – no, don't endanger, don't endanger yourself – but you'd say six metres, maybe, twenty foot, perhaps – hello – hello –

SARIKA. Right, right, hullo, no, this isn't, I mean, we don't – I've lost you again – is this a mobile, okay, your signal – no, you're back again, better, oh, so you're driving, I see, okay, you shouldn't really – of course, what sort of speed what –

I meant the waves, actually the – okay, Tessa, sorry, I need to – what? Tessa – this is, this person's on the A52, which is – I will alert, if I can get through – is there anyone else there?

Right. And are they on higher ground? There must be some higher ground.

*Suddenly all power goes, all light goes, the screen goes,
everything; somewhere off an alarm sounds.*

SARIKA. Hello –

CHRIS. This is – what is – ?

TESSA. Oh – gone – gone –

WILL. What is this – they –

SARIKA. This is – this shouldn't – really –

CHRIS. What, what is fucking happening here?

TESSA. I'll go, go and see.

WILL. Maybe it's a substation gone.

SARIKA. Couldn't have reached Sizewell or –

CHRIS. It shouldn't be affecting us, for Christ's sake – we're –

WILL. Incredible wind speeds, power lines –

TESSA. Who, who supplies us with – energy?

SARIKA. EDF. I think. I don't know.

CHRIS. EDF! I've got shares in fucking EDF.

WILL. EDF, E.ON, whatever, they've probably lost loads of
capacity and when they –

CHRIS. Don't we have a back-up generator?

SARIKA. We must do, I am sure we do –

TESSA. Oh, this is ludicrous.

CHRIS. How are we supposed to do our jobs in the dark?

TESSA. Is there light in the corridor even – ?

SARIKA. No street lights.

Pause.

CHRIS. Guy on the phone sounded – terrified.

So much noise in the background, kind of, I don't know,
sucking sound, like tinnitus, like I was inside my own ear.

SARIKA. It was a woman. Alone in a car.

I don't think it was a hands-free.

I heard that sound too. Yes.

Like water going down a plughole.

TESSA. You get the impression it's not proceeding in an orderly fashion there.

WILL. Not really, no.

TESSA. It's a little early to draw conclusions…

SARIKA. Where's this back-up?

WILL. Have you tried your mobiles, say?

SARIKA. Hang on.

TESSA. Nothing, nothing on mine.

CHRIS. Could use it as a light at least.

SARIKA. Mmm.

She plays it around them. It fades out. She does it again.

WILL. You'll waste your battery.

Pause.

CHRIS. Well. How powerful are you feeling right now, Tessa?

TESSA. Not very.

CHRIS. Oh God. Am I supposed to, what, fly to King's Lynn? In this sort of –

SARIKA. We should probably rethink that.

CHRIS. Yeah. Yeah.

TESSA. I'll go and get –

SARIKA. I don't think you can.

TESSA. What?

SARIKA. I think – the door. No. Oh dear.

TESSA. Can you light it –

SARIKA. It's the swipe-card system.

CHRIS. Oh no, oh no, you must be kidding.

SARIKA. I don't think you can override it.

WILL. Do they not have an override?

SARIKA. Externally. Remember, even the loos are smart-flush.

CHRIS. Jesus wept. Can't even take a dump without a computer.

TESSA. Surely we can force it?

SARIKA. It's designed to be a robust door.

CHRIS. The Ministry of Cock-Up.

The Minister of Fuck-Up.

TESSA. Christopher. Brace up.

Pause. WILL's laughing.

WILL. This is – ridiculous. Isn't it?

SARIKA. That's hardly helpful, Will.

WILL. Sorry. Sorry. It's just, you imagine it, you imagine power from the outside, you imagine how invulnerable it is.

CHRIS. That's the kind of sixth-form insight we've come to expect from you.

Suddenly a strange, faint scratching sound from the inner door.

SARIKA. Listen!

TESSA. Ah, yes.

SARIKA. Maybe it's security – hello!

CHRIS. We're in here. Hurry it along!

SARIKA. Funny.

It's not the outer door, it's from my office.

CHRIS. Just get yourself in here, can't you.

SARIKA. Hello!

Just come in.

The door opens and light sweeps through the darkness.

CHRIS. Who is that? Declare yourself.

TESSA. At least they have a light.

It's JENKS, *his light mounted on his bike helmet. He laughs.*

JENKS. Oh dear. The commanding heights of the state.

WILL. Colin. What is – ?

CHRIS. Who authorised you to – ?

SARIKA. What were you doing in my office?

JENKS. Sorry.

Left my helmet in there.

Never got to pick it up.

SARIKA. You still have the key?

JENKS. It seems to function. You could get out from there into the corridor.

CHRIS. Get that light out of my face.

JENKS. Hang on. Sorry. Okay.

He takes his helmet off.

You should see London out there.

No lights in all directions. You could see the stars. Were it not for the occluded fronts. Like the Blitz.

Father walking me along Millbank in the blackout. Sensing the river through the smog. The city like a great black beast.

I suspect the back-up generators will kick in soon. But you do fear for those in surgery.

He places his halogen light on the table and it offers a cold, watery illumination.

WILL. What… what are you doing here anyway?

JENKS. Oh. Am I at liberty to say, Tessa?

Pause.

TESSA. Colin and I have remained in communication.

CHRIS. Right. News to me. News to you, Sarika?

SARIKA. Yes.

TESSA. I am Minister for Resilience after all. I liaise with the MOD, Intelligence.

The MOD have shown great interest in certain ideas, certain engineering solutions Colin's been tinkering with.

CHRIS. Are you hatching some sort… of fucking coup here?

TESSA. Please don't try the alpha-male act on me, Christopher, I'm really not susceptible to bullying.

CHRIS. You've been undermining me at all levels, haven't you.

TESSA. I think you made a pretty good job of undermining yourself, Christopher.

CHRIS. You mendacious – bitch –

TESSA. Oh, you're really going to regret saying that.

CHRIS. Shafting me, fucking me over and over –

TESSA. Stop this –

CHRIS. So you want my ministry for your own pathetic little purposes!

Turning us all into Sister fucking Wendy.

You want your own ministry?

TESSA. I don't think that's in either of our gifts, is it, any more?

The lights flicker on, the phones emit a low drone.

JENKS. At last. The whole Heath Robinson mechanism stutters into life.

CHRIS. Get out of my ministry.

Consider yourself fired, from now!

TESSA. Christopher, I think you need to calm down and give some serious thought to your position –

CHRIS. You clear your desk.

SARIKA. You can't actually do this, Chris.

CHRIS. You clear your desk.

TESSA. Let's run it past David.

CHRIS. He can clear his fucking desk too.

TESSA. This is becoming embarrassing.

SARIKA. Chris, stop it, stop it now.

CHRIS. What?

SARIKA. Stop this right now, what you're doing.

CHRIS. What?

SARIKA. Stop it.

He looks at her, dazed. The alarm stops.

CHRIS. Right. Okay. Yes.

Pause.

TESSA. What we should be concerning ourselves with now is the outside world.

WILL. Do you know what happened to East Anglia?

JENKS. I don't think anyone really knows, do they.

The phones all begin to ring again. They ignore them.

CHRIS. Tessa, what I just said –

TESSA. I suggest you and I go and see David.

CHRIS. Right. To what end?

TESSA. To clarify your position.

CHRIS. Right. Because of how –

TESSA. Because you countermanded my order.

Because you revoked one evacuation and delayed others to, I presume, fatal effect.

CHRIS. Right.

TESSA. Now, look, off you go, I'll follow on.

CHRIS. Okay. Okay.

He lingers during this next dialogue.

TESSA. Sarika, set in process the contingency plan as agreed on.

SARIKA. For what, for which regions?

TESSA. West Norfolk, albeit belatedly.

East Norfolk. Suffolk. Essex.

Kent-Essex borders. Canvey Island.

The Medway. Wallingsea.

Lewisham, Greenwich, Isle of Dogs, Canary Wharf –

SARIKA. Bermondsey, Rotherhithe, the City –

WILL. Chelsea, Battersea –

CHRIS. Suddenly you notice all the 'seas'.

Now SARIKA*'s on the phone, her lines running through the next lines.*

SARIKA. Sarika Chatterjee. Yes. Activate evacuation plan. Yes.

Yes – do we have a situation report, for, say, let's say, Hunstanton: okay – how bad. Right.

WILL. Can I hear that – can I –

SARIKA. But mostly cleared –

She waves him away.

Evacuation Station A: Swaffham.

Evacuation Station B: Diss.

Evacuation Station C: Norwich.

Evacuation Station D: Ipswich.

Evacuation Station E: Colchester.

CHRIS. I mean, what would Nelson do? In this situation?

TESSA. Nelson wouldn't be in this situation.

Go and see David.

CHRIS. No. That's the thing. Nelson wouldn't be in this situation.

He galvanises himself to go but can't.

TESSA. Colin, I think what we'll need in Triple C is some kind of emergency engineering. Scuttling vessels in estuary mouths. Dropping hard core into coastal waters. Thoughts about helicopter deployment.

I'll join you after signing off with David.

JENKS. Yes. Very good.

TESSA. Okay, Christopher. Let's go.

CHRIS. Right. Lead on.

They go. SARIKA *alone with* WILL *and* JENKS; *her text is repeated through their dialogue.*

SARIKA. A10: Southbound only, both lanes.

A14: Westbound only, both lanes.

A12: Westbound only, both lanes.

A11: Westbound only, both lanes.

A143: Westbound only, both lanes.

A133: Closed.

A28: Closed.

A127: Westbound only, both lanes.

No, I can't repeat the bloody list.

Sorry. Sorry.

JENKS. I expect you're thinking about your parents?

WILL. I don't really want to discuss this.

JENKS. That's understandable.

> But I wanted to say I've come to understand I did Rob a very great wrong. I did want to say that to you. He was, he is a very fine scientist.

WILL. I should have stayed. Should have completed my work.

JENKS. The reality of Government is often disappointing. But I always think the key thing is to imagine them without us.

> How would they fare then?

WILL. What the fuck am I doing here?

JENKS. This won't happen again. I mean, we're talking about how we might artfully and permanently engineer the worst impacts away from our shores. Giant sluice gates at the head of all our estuaries keep out sea levels, and in the process, enable better migration control.

> An arm cradled around the whole nation. Inspiring.

> So perhaps I ought to thank you.

> For sending me back to the science.

> Right. Triple C.

> Don't be hard on yourself, William.

> You acted in good faith.

He goes. SARIKA *and* WILL *are left alone.*

SARIKA. I'm sorry.

WILL. What?

SARIKA. Hunstanton and environs, apparently, hit by very severe waves.

> No indication of fatalities as yet.

> The likelihood is they got out, have holed up with friends –

WILL. They don't have any.

SARIKA. Will, don't be lugubrious.

WILL. I should have done something different here but I really don't know what it is.

TESSA *enters*.

TESSA. Sarika, you're needed in Triple C.

SARIKA. Right. You – you gonna be okay, Will?

TESSA. Immediately.

WILL. Oh. Yeah, I'm great, I'm good.

Go do your duty.

TESSA. Thank you.

SARIKA *starts to go*.

You're working for me now.

Subject to your performance tonight.

I know you don't like me.

But that's not an issue for me, actually.

But if you're working for me I don't tolerate any abuse of procedure, especially of a personal nature.

Do you understand me?

SARIKA *looks at* WILL.

Do you understand me?

SARIKA *nods and goes*.

WILL. You must be feeling pretty chuffed.

TESSA. Now why do you say that?

WILL. We failed the big test, didn't we?

Original sin all over again.

TESSA. I don't have time for a theological exchange.

She pulls a document from her bag.

I took the liberty of carving out a potential post for you.

It's rare, of course, for a figure such as yourself to get a Parliamentary seat.

But there are ministerial roles, and anyway, I think we might start to rethink all of that after tonight.

I would think we might be considering a new sort of Government altogether, a Government of National Unity, the expert empowered, protected from public scrutiny, the full force of the law in their gift.

WILL. I see. With you in charge.

TESSA. David's aware he made a very grave error of judgement tonight.

But frankly I'm more interested in the efficacy of my role than public visibility.

You'll need a little time to think about it.

WILL. What, if I may say, what I find, I don't know, unseemly, is you seem – well, excited.

TESSA. Well, I find all this salutary. It puts us back in our place. A salutary lesson in human limitation, I think.

WILL. You're a very strange person, Tessa.

TESSA. My sentiments are less uncommon than you imagine.

She starts to go.

Did I ever say I met your father?

WILL. What?

TESSA. I was a Civil Servant in the Ministry of Science and Education.

When he came to us, I remember vividly the things he said. He was a crank, of course. But his ideas… stayed with me.

WILL. No, you didn't, you didn't say that.

Pause.

Do you want my response in writing?

TESSA. E-mail's fine.

She goes. WILL *alone. He tries the phones.*

WILL. 01485 792264.

I can wait. Yep.

So, no – no connection. Right.

Okay. Thank you. Thanks.

He stares at the phone.

SARIKA *re-enters; she looks shaken.*

What?

SARIKA. I – well, I got this – text.

WILL. What? What text?

SARIKA. Weird. All capitals. 'SEA ROB NO.'

WILL. S-E-E?

SARIKA. S-E-A.

He reads it.

WILL. 'SEA ROB NO.'

SARIKA. Tried to call it and there wasn't – there was –

WILL. 'SEA ROB NO.'

When's the – what's the time on it?

SARIKA. Forty minutes ago. Before the –

WILL. And you rang it?

SARIKA. Nothing.

WILL takes the phone, tries to call. Nothing.

WILL. Is this her number?

SARIKA. I think it is. I think it's your –

WILL. 'SEA ROB NO.'

SARIKA. I'm so sorry, love.

She holds him; he simply shakes uncontrollably.

Sssh. Sssh. Sssh.

It doesn't confirm –

It doesn't – it might mean –

It's okay.

The phones ring again.

The thing is, they want me in Triple C.

They need to know about London.

In Triple C.

She releases him.

The thing is, I have to answer that.

I really have to answer that.

Pause.

WILL. Yeah. Okay.

SARIKA. So. London?

WILL stands; the phone rings; SARIKA stands.

Suddenly the sound of an enormous storm.

Blackout.

The End.

A Nick Hern Book

The Contingency Plan first published in Great Britain in 2009 as a
paperback original by Nick Hern Books Limited, 14 Larden Road,
London W3 7ST, in association with the Bush Theatre, London

The Contingency Plan copyright © Steve Waters

Steve Waters has asserted his moral right to be identified as the author
of this work

Cover image: aka
Cover design: Ned Hoste, 2H

Typeset by Nick Hern Books, London

Printed in the UK by CPI Antony Rowe, Chippenham, Wiltshire

A CIP catalogue record for this book is available from the British Library

ISBN 978 1 84842 052 6

FSC

Mixed Sources
Product group from well-managed
forests and other controlled sources

Cert no. SGS-COC-2953
www.fsc.org
© 1996 Forest Stewardship Council

bushfutures

bushfutures is a groundbreaking programme that allows our community, emerging practitioners and playwrights to access the expertise of Bush writers, directors, designers, technicians and actors.

We are devoted to finding and supporting the Bush artists of tomorrow.

bushfutures **Projects**

bushfutures creates exciting and innovative projects to engage new playwrights and put their writing on the Bush stage. In 2008 projects included **The Halo Project** and **50 Ways to Leave Your Lover**, a sell-out show harnessing the talents of five exciting young playwrights which toured to several theatres as well as Latitude Festival. This year's Latitude show is **suddenlossofdignity.com** by Zawe Ashton, James Graham, Joel Horwood, Morgan Lloyd Malcolm and Michelle Terry, which will tour to Plymouth, Bath, Bristol and finish with a run at the Bush from 29 July–15 August. To insure your dignity against loss and contribute stories to inspire our playwrights, go to www.suddenlossofidgnity.com.

bushfutures **in schools and the community**

bushfutures develops projects with schools, colleges and community groups. As one of Britain's leading new writing companies, we share our talent and expertise with young people through tailor-made workshops which focus on playwriting, performance and the development of new work.

A Night Less Ordinary

Under 26? Like getting a freebie? Then you've come to the right place. As part of a new national scheme, the Bush is offering free theatre tickets to those aged 25 and under (one free ticket available per person per year)*. So if you fancy A Night Less Ordinary and want to see some of the best new shows in London call our friendly box office on 020 8743 5050 for more details and to book tickets.

BushPush

No need to worry if you have used your A Night Less Ordinary ticket for the year, you can continue to see the Bush's great work for a mere £7.50*. This offer is available to everyone aged 25 and under and full-time students for all previews on every production staged at the Bush. Please quote **BushPush** when booking and bring ID for ticket collection.

Want to get involved? Go to
www.bushtheatre.co.uk/bushfutures
to find out how

* subject to availability

Be there at the beginning

Our work identifying and nurturing playwrights is only made possible through the generous support of our Patrons and other donors. Thank you to all those who have supported us during the last year.

If you are interested in finding out how to be involved, please visit the 'Support Us' section of www.bushtheatre.co.uk, or call 020 8743 3584.

At the Bush Theatre

Artistic Director	**Josie Rourke**
Producer	**Angela Bond**
Associate Director **bush**futures	**Anthea Williams**
Associate Director	**James Grieve**
Finance Manager	**Viren Thakker**
Marketing Manager	**Stephanie Hui**
Production Manager	**Sam Craven-Griffiths**
Assistant Producer	**Caroline Dyott**
Artists' Administrator	**Tara Wilkinson**
Acting Development Managers	**Poppy Ben-David** **Leonora Twynam**
Assistant Administrator	**Natasha Bloor**
Box Office Supervisor	**Clare Moss**
Box Office Assistants	**Natasha Bloor, Kirsty Cox,** **Asha Jennings Grant, Alex Hern,** **Ava Leman Morgan, Lee Maxwell Simpson**
Front of House Duty Managers	**Kellie Batchelor, Rachel Boulton,** **Euan Forsyth, Alex Hern,** **Oliver Lavery, Ava Leman Morgan,** **Sam Plumb, Rose Romain,** **Lois Tucker**
Duty Technicians	**Deb Jones, Sara Macleod,** **Ben Sherratt, Clare Spillman,** **Matthew Vile**
Associate Artists	**Tanya Burns, Arthur Darvill,** **Chloe Emmerson, James Farncombe,** **Richard Jordan, Emma Laxton,** **Paul Miller, Lucy Osborne**
Associate Playwright	**Anthony Weigh**
Creative Associates	**Nathan Curry, Charlotte Gwinner,** **Clare Lizzimore, George Perrin,** **Hamish Pirie, Dawn Walton**
Writer in Residence	**Jack Thorne**
Press Representative	**Ewan Thomson**
Resident Assistant Director	**Hannah Ashwell-Dickinson**
Intern	**Victoria Featherby**

The Bush Theatre
Shepherds Bush Green
London W12 8QD

Box Office: 020 8743 5050
www.bushtheatre.co.uk

The Alternative Theatre Company Ltd. (The Bush Theatre)
is a Registered Charity number: 270080
Co. registration number 1221968 | VAT no. 228 3168 73

supported by

The Bush Theatre

'One of the most experienced prospectors of raw talent in Europe'
The Independent

For thirty-nine years, the Bush Theatre has pursued its singular vision of discovery, risk and entertainment from its home in Shepherds Bush. That vision is valued and embraced by a community of audience and artists radiating out from our distinctive corner of West London across the world. The Bush is a local theatre with an international reputation. Since its inception, the Bush has produced hundreds of groundbreaking premieres, many of them Bush commissions, and hosted guest productions by leading companies and artists from across the world. On any given night, those queuing at the foot of our stairs to take their seats could have travelled from Auckland or popped in from round the corner.

What draws them to the Bush is the promise of a good night out and our proven commitment to launch, from our stage, successive generations of playwrights and artists. Samuel Adamson, David Eldridge, Jonathan Harvey, Catherine Johnson, Tony Kushner, Stephen Poliakoff, Jack Thorne and Victoria Wood (all then unknown) began their careers at the Bush. The unwritten contract between talent and risk is understood by actors who work at the Bush, creating roles in untested new plays. Unique amongst local theatres, the Bush consistently draws actors of the highest reputation and calibre. Joseph Fiennes and Ian Hart recently took leading roles in a first play by an unknown playwright to great critical success. John Simm and Richard Wilson acted in premieres both of which transferred into the West End. The Bush has won over 100 awards, and developed an enviable reputation for touring its acclaimed productions nationally and internationally.

Audiences and organisations far beyond our stage profit from the risks we take. The value attached to the Bush by other theatres and by the film and television industries is both significant and considerable. The Bush receives more than 1,000 scripts through the post every year, and reads and responds to them all. This is one small part of a comprehensive playwrights' development programme which nurtures the relationship between writer and director, as well as playwright residencies and commissions. Everything that we do to develop playwrights focuses them towards a production on our stage or beyond.

We have also launched an ambitious new education, training and professional development programme, **bush**futures, providing opportunities for different sectors of the community and professionals to access the expertise of Bush playwrights, directors, designers, technicians and actors, and to play an active role in influencing the future development of the theatre and its programme. Over the next three years we aim to increase the reach and impact of the work we do by seeking out and developing networks for writers using digital technology and the internet. Through this pioneering work, the Bush will reach and connect with new writers and new audiences.

Josie Rourke
Artistic Director

Verity Sadler Assistant Designer

Verity graduated in Theatre Design in 2008 at the Royal Welsh College of Music and Drama.

Theatre includes: as assistant to Sean Crowley, *The Thorn Birds* (Theatre Wales), *She Stoops to Conquer* (Torch/Mappa Mundi); as assistant to Tom Scutt, *Edward Gant's Amazing Feats of Loneliness* (Headlong), *Unbroken* (Gate, London); as a scenic painter, *Neville's Island*, *Cinderella* (Torch).

Film includes: art department, *Mr Nice* (Independent Film Company).

Tom Scutt Designer

Theatre includes: *Edward Gant's Amazing Feats of Loneliness* (Headlong); *Unbroken*, *The Internationalist* (Gate, London); *Bay* (Young Vic); *The Merchant of Venice* (Octagon, nominated for the Manchester Evening News Best Design Award 2008); *Metropolis* (Theatre Royal, Bath); *The Observer* (design consultant, National Theatre Studio); *Paradise Lost* (Southwark Playhouse); *Mad Funny Just* (Old Vic New Voices Award winner 2008); *The Water Harvest* (Theatre503); *Return* (Watford Palace); *The Comedy of Errors* (RSC); *Skellig* (onO Productions); *Loaded* (Fireraisers).

Forthcoming work includes: *After Miss Julie* (Salisbury Playhouse).

For his work with Headlong Theatre, Tom was awarded the 2007 Linbury Biennial Prize and the Jocelyn Herbert Award for Stage Design.

Francesca Seeley Assistant Director

Francesca trained as a director with Living Pictures and studied English and Italian literature at the University of York.

Theatre includes: as director, *Comp* (Tristan Bates); *Now I Wonder What You Are* (Greenwich Playhouse); as assistant director, *The Long Road* (Soho Theatre); *Tagged to a Number*, with prisoners and ex-prisoners (Synergy Theatre Project schools tour/BAC).

Francesca is co-Artistic Director of Nameless Theatre, which produces *One Night Stands* – a monthly series of rehearsed readings of new writing.

Steve Waters Writer

Writing for theatre includes: *Fast Labour* (Hampstead, in association with West Yorkshire Playhouse); *Out of Your Knowledge* (Menagerie Theatre/Pleasance, Edinburgh/East Anglian tour); *World Music* (Sheffield Crucible, and subsequent transfer to the Donmar Warehouse); *The Unthinkable* (Sheffield Crucible); *English Journeys*, *After the Gods* (Hampstead); a translation/ adaptation of a new play by Philippe Minyana, *Habitats* (Gate, London/Tron, Glasgow); *Flight Without End* (LAMDA).

Writing for TV and Radio includes: *Safe House* (BBC4) and *The Moderniser* (BBC Radio 4).

Steve runs the Birmingham MPhil in Playwriting. He is a member of the British Theatre Consortium.

Globe); *The Strangeness of Others, Odysseus* (RADA); *Sitting Pretty* (Watford Palace); *Romeo and Juliet, The Golden Ass* (University of South Florida, USA); *Markings* (Southwark Playhouse/Traverse, Edinburgh); *The Graduate* (UK tour); *A Tempestade* (associate director, Teatro Sao Luiz, Portugal); *Young Emma, Something Cloudy, Something Clear* (Finborough); *The Lion, the Witch and the Wardrobe* (Maitisong, Botswana); as co-director, *Hamlet* (The Factory). In the West End, she has directed *Whipping It Up* (Olivier Award nominee, Best New Comedy, from the original production at the Bush by Terry Johnson) and co-directed *One Flew Over the Cuckoo's Nest* (2005 and 2006).

Forthcoming work includes: *Bedroom Farce* (West Yorkshire Playhouse).

Tamara was one of the directors of the 24 Hour Plays at the Old Vic in 2007 and 2008. She is an Artistic Associate for Theatre of Memory and a Trustee of the Peggy Ramsay Foundation.

Emma Laxton Sound Designer

Theatre for the Bush includes: *Wrecks, Broken Space Season, 2000 Feet Away, Tinderbox.*

Theatre for the Royal Court includes: *Tusk Tusk, Faces in the Crowd, That Face, Gone Too Far!, Catch, Scenes from the Back of Beyond, Woman and Scarecrow, The World's Biggest Diamond, Incomplete and Random Acts of Kindness, My Name Is Rachel Corrie* (also Minetta Lane, New York/Galway Festival/Edinburgh Festival), *Bone, The Weather, Bear Hug, Terrorism, Food Chain.* West End theatre includes: *Treasure Island* (Theatre Royal, Haymarket); *That Face* (Duke Of York's); *My Name Is Rachel Corrie* (Playhouse).

Other theatre includes: *A Christmas Carol* (Chichester); *Welcome to Ramallah* (Ice and Fire); *Pornography* (Birmingham Rep/Traverse, Edinburgh); *Shoot/Get Treasure/Repeat* (National Theatre); *Europe* (Dundee Rep/Barbican Pit); *Other Hands* (Soho Theatre); *The Unthinkable* (Sheffield Crucible); *My Dad is a Birdman* (Young Vic); *The Gods Are Not to Blame* (Arcola).

Michael Longhurst Director – *On the Beach*

Michael trained in directing at Mountview after reading Philosophy at Nottingham University.

Theatre for the Bush includes: *Stovepipe* (HighTide in collaboration with the National Theatre).

Other theatre includes: *dirty butterfly* (Young Vic); *1 in 5* (Daring Pairings, Hampstead); *The Death of Cool* (Tristan Bates); *New Voices: 24 Hour Plays* (Old Vic); *Gaudeamus* (Arcola); *Guardians* (Pleasance, Edinburgh/ Theatre503); *Cargo* (Pleasance, Edinburgh/Oval House); *Doctor Faustus* (Djanogly, Lakeside Nottingham). As Assistant Director: *A Respectable Wedding* (Young Vic); *Gaslight* (Old Vic); *The Family Plays* (Royal Court).

Michael received the 2007 Jerwood Directors Award for *dirty butterfly* at the Young Vic. His 2005 Fringe First-winning production of *Guardians* was recently included as part of the *This is War* exhibition at the Barbican Art Gallery.

Hannah Ashwell-Dickinson Associate Director

Hannah is Resident Assistant Director at the Bush and is currently studying for an MFA in Theatre Directing at Birkbeck College.

Theatre for the Bush includes: *Wrecks, St Petersburg, Two Cigarettes, Little Dolls, Turf*.

Other assistant directing work includes: *The List* (Arcola); *Vassa, A Servant to Two Masters* (RADA); *Marvellous Animals, Saxophone* (Tristan Bates/OTC readings).

Forthcoming work includes: *Apologia* (as Assistant Director, the Bush).

Oliver Fenwick Lighting Designer

Theatre includes: *Mary Stewart* (Hipp Theatre, Sweden); *Hedda Gabler* (Gate, Dublin); *Happy Now?* (National Theatre); *Private Lives, The Giant, Glass Eels, Comfort Me With Apples* (Hampstead); *Endgame* (Liverpool Everyman); *Far From the Madding Crowd* (ETT tour); *The Lady from the Sea, She Stoops to Conquer, On the Piste* (Birmingham Rep); *The Elephant Man* (Lycium Sheffield and tour); *Kean* (Apollo, West End); *Jack and the Beanstalk* (Barbican); *Pure Gold* (Soho Theatre) *Henry V, Mirandolina, A Conversation* (Royal Exchange); *Terms of Endearment* (tour); *Restoration* (Bristol Old Vic and tour for Headlong); *My Fair Lady* (Cameron Mackintosh/National Theatre tour); *The Caretaker* (Tricycle); *The Comedy of Errors, Bird Calls, Iphigenia* (Sheffield Crucible); *A Doll's House* (West Yorkshire Playhouse); *Sunshine on Leith* (Dundee Rep and tour); *Heartbreak House* (Watford Palace); *A Model Girl* (Greenwich); *The Solid Gold Cadillac* (Garrick, West End); *The Secret Rapture* (Lyric, West End); *Noises Off, All My Sons, Doctor Faustus* (Liverpool Playhouse); *The Chairs* (Gate, London); *Follies, Insignificance, Breaking the Code* (Theatre Royal, Northampton); *Tartuffe, The Gentleman from Olmedo, The Venetian Twins, Hobson's Choice, Dancing at Lughnasa, Love in a Maze* (Watermill); *Fields of Gold, Villette* (Stephen Joseph); *Cinderella* (Bristol Old Vic); *Hysteria, Children of a Lesser God* (Salisbury Playhouse).

Opera includes: *Samson et Delilah, Lohengrin* (Royal Opera House); *The Trojan Trilogy, The Nose* (Linbury ROH); *The Gentle Giant* (The Clore ROH); *The Threepenny Opera* (The Opera Group); *L'Opera Seria* (Batignano Festival).

Tamara Harvey Director – *Resilience*

Tamara is a graduate of the University of Bristol and trained at the Shakespeare Theatre of New Jersey, USA.

Theatre for the Bush includes: *tHe dYsFUnCKshOnalZ!* (nominated for Best Off-West End Production, Whatsonstage Awards).

Other theatre includes: *Plague Over England* (Finborough, nominated for Best Off-West End Production, Whatsonstage Awards and the subsequent West End production); *Romeo and Juliet* (Theatre of Memory at Middle Temple Hall); *Grand Slam, Who's the Daddy?* (King's Head); *Rock* (tour); *Touch Wood, Purvis, Storm in a Tea Chest, The Prodigal Son* (Stephen Joseph); *Closer* (Theatre Royal, Northampton); *One Flew Over the Cuckoo's Nest* (UK tour); *Bash* (Trafalgar Studios); *An Hour and a Half Late* (Theatre Royal Bath and UK tour); *The Importance of Being Earnest* (Shakespeare Theatre of New Jersey, USA); *Much Ado About Nothing* (Shakespeare's

Stephanie Street Sarika

Stephanie trained at LAMDA and studied English at Cambridge University.

Theatre includes: *Shades* (Royal Court); *The Scarecrow and his Servant* (Southwark); *Sweet Cider* (Arcola); *Too Close to Home* (Lyric); *The Laramie Project* (Kit Productions); *The Vagina Monologues* (UK tour); *Dark Meaning Mouse* (Finborough); *Strictly Dandia* (Tamasha Theatre Company); *As You Like It* (Greenwich Observatory); *Arabian Nights* (ATC Productions).

TV includes: *Monday Monday, Apparitions, Holby City, Never Better, EastEnders, Primeval, Commander III, Soundproof, Coming Up 2005, Heavenly Father, Nylon, Doctors, Twenty Things to Do Before You're Thirty, Red Cap, The Last Detective.*

Robin Soans Robin / Jenks

Theatre includes: *Coriolanus, Under the Black Flag* (Shakespeare's Globe); *Love's Labour's Lost, Anything Goes, A Prayer for Owen Meany, Volpone, The London Cuckolds, The Invention of Love* (National Theatre); *On Ego, Jump Mr Malinoff Jump* (Soho Theatre); *The Holy Terror* (Duke of York's and tour); *Push Up, Shopping and Fucking, Waiting Room Germany, Stargazy Pie and Sauerkraut, Three Birds Alighting on a Field, Etta Jenks, Bed of Roses* (Royal Court); *Hamlet* (Young Vic); *Ghosts* (Comedy, West End); *Another Country* (The Arts); *The Positive Hour* (Hampstead and tour); *The Country Wife, The Venetian Twins, Murder in the Cathedral* (RSC); *Walpurgis Night* (Gate, London); *Hamlet, Woyzeck* (Half Moon); *Dead Funny* (Watford Palace); *The Rivals* (Nottingham Playhouse); *Fashion, Thatcher's Women* (Tricycle).

TV includes: *Waking the Dead, Midsomer Murders, Holby City, Miss Marple, Not Only But Always, The Russian Bride, Dalziel and Pascoe, Dangerfield, Kavanagh QC, Far from the Madding Crowd, Jonathan Creek, Rebecca, Inspector Morse, Bergerac, Tales of Sherwood Forest, Dr Who.*

Film includes: *The Queen, Pierrepoint, Method, The God Club, AKA, Sabotage, Comrades, Absolution, The Patricia Neal Story, Hidden City, Blue Juice.*

As a playwright: *The Arab Israeli Cookbook* (Gate, London; revived at the Tricycle, London and in the USA, Canada and Japan); *Talking to Terrorists* (Out of Joint production at the Royal Court and on UK tour and in the USA); *A State Affair* (Out of Joint production at Soho Theatre; two national tours; invited performance at the House of Lords); *Life After Scandal* (Hampstead).

Geoffrey Streatfeild Will

Geoffrey trained at RADA and studied Drama at Manchester University.

Theatre includes: *Henry VI Parts 1, 2 and 3, Henry V, Henry IV Parts 1 and 2, Richard III* (RSC); *The History Boys, Bacchae* (National Theatre); *Journey's End* (West End); *The Merchant of Venice, Nathan the Wise* (Chichester).

TV includes: *Hunter, Elizabeth I, Twenty Thousand Streets Under the Sky, Midsomer Murders, The Other Boleyn Girl, Love in a Cold Climate, Sword of Honour.*

Film includes: *Angel, Match Point, Kinky Boots.*

David Bark-Jones Chris

Theatre includes: *The Way of the World* (Theatre Royal and Derngate, Northampton); *The Forest, Machinal, Arcadia* (National Theatre); *Schippel the Plumber* (Watford Palace); *Julius Caesar* (Birmingham Rep); *All's Well That Ends Well* (Royal Exchange); *Some Sunny Day* (Hampstead); *Venice Preserved* (Almeida); *Dealer's Choice* (National Theatre/Vaudeville); *Les Liaisons Dangereuses* (Wolsey, Ipswich); *She Stoops to Conquer* (Derby Playhouse).

TV includes: *New Tricks, Slings and Arrows, Wilson, No Angels, Rosemary and Thyme, Life for Daniel, Rough Treatment, Oliver Twist, Bramwell, A Wing and a Prayer, The Legacy of Reggie Perrin, Pride and Prejudice, Press Gang, Trainer.*

Film includes: *The Calling, RocknRolla, Sixty Six, The Da Vinci Code, A Gentle Creature* (short).

Susan Brown Jenny / Tessa

Theatre includes: *Harper Regan, The Hour We Knew Nothing of Each Other, Playing With Fire, Henry IV Parts 1 and 2, Cardiff East* (National Theatre); *Easter, Romeo and Juliet, Richard III, Bad Weather* (RSC); *Road, Shirley, Downfall, Gibraltar Strait, Seagulls* (Royal Court); *Dying For It, Butterfly Kiss* (Almeida); *The Wild Duck* (Donmar Warehouse); *The Chairs, The House of Bernarda Alba* (Gate, London); *You Be Ted and I'll Be Sylvia* (Hampstead); *The Beaux Stratagem, Back to Methuselah, The Vortex, The Way of the World, A Woman of No Importance* (Cambridge Theatre Company); *Playing Sinatra* (The Warehouse/Greenwich); *Twelfth Night* (English Touring Theatre); *Small Change, Iphigenia* (Sheffield Crucible).

TV includes: *Road* (Winner Prix Italia), *Loving Hazel, Making Out, Absolute Hell, Nona, Prime Suspect, The Riff Raff Element, September Song, A Touch of Frost, Taggart, Wokenwell, Anorak of Fire, The Vice, Wire in the Blood, The Best of Both Worlds, Blue Dove, Dalziel and Pascoe, Brides in the Bath, La Femme Musketeer, Rose and Maloney, Pinochet in Suburbia, Torchwood* (to be screened in June).

Film includes: *Brideshead Revisited, Hope and Glory.*

Radio includes: *Number 10, Felix Holt the Radical.*

Cast

Chris	**David Bark-Jones**
Jenny / Tessa	**Susan Brown**
Robin / Jenks	**Robin Soans**
Will	**Geoffrey Streatfeild**
Sarika	**Stephanie Street**

Writer	**Steve Waters**
Director – *On the Beach*	**Michael Longhurst**
Director – *Resilience*	**Tamara Harvey**
Associate Director	**Hannah Ashwell-Dickinson**
Designer	**Tom Scutt**
Lighting Designer	**Oliver Fenwick**
Sound Designer	**Emma Laxton**
Assistant Director	**Francesca Seeley**
Assistant Designer	**Verity Sadler**
Resident Stage Manager	**Angela Riddell**
Deputy Stage Manager – *On the Beach*	**Dave Blakemore**
Deputy Stage Manager – *Resilience*	**Charlotte Heath**

The Bush Theatre would like to give particular thanks to AKA and to West 12 Shopping Centre; and would like to thank E J Barnes Cycles, Brompton Bikes, discountcoffee.co.uk, hurricanelamps.co.uk, KA Seafood, Metropolitan Police, Morrisons, The Real Greek (Westfield Centre), Samsonite Black Label (available at House of Fraser, Westfield Centre), Siemens, WWT London Wetland Centre and the Young Vic Theatre Company.

The Contingency Plan received its world premiere on 22 April 2009.

bush theatre

The Bush Theatre presents the world premiere of

The Contingency Plan

by Steve Waters

22 April – 6 June 2009